Judith Wills

100 Favourite
SLIM & HEALTHY
Recipes

JUDITH WILLS

100 Favourite
SLIM & HEALTHY
Recipes

PIATKUS

First published in 1996 by
Judy Piatkus (Publishers) Ltd
5 Windmill Street, London W1P 1HF

First paperback edition 1997

The moral right of the author has been asserted

A catalogue record for this book is available from the British Library

ISBN 0–7499–1541–2 (hbk)
ISBN 0–7499–1673–7 (pbk)

Designed by Paul Saunders
Photographs by Martin Brigdale
Food for photography prepared by Meg Jansz
Photographic styling by Helen Trent

Typeset by Phoenix Photosetting, Chatham, Kent
Printed and bound in Great Britain by
Butler & Tanner Ltd, Frome, Somerset

CONTENTS

INTRODUCTION

I love to cook. I love to eat. And I like to think that what I eat is setting me up for as healthy, strong and long a future as possible. But I am not – absolutely *not* – a 'health food freak'; I don't believe that eating for health and eating for enjoyment necessarily have to be two completely different things.

This book is about cooking meals that taste good; that you really want to prepare and eat; and that also happen to be good for your health, and your waistline, too. In the chapters that follow, you will find plenty of what most people think of as 'healthy foods' – masses of vegetables, fish, pasta, grains, even the odd beansprout and portion of brown rice – but you will *also* find beef, cheese, eggs, desserts, and even butter and sugar. None of these can fairly be described as 'unhealthy', but many, many people *do* think of them as 'bad' foods. The fact is that there is no one food that is 'healthy' or 'unhealthy' – only a diet that is healthily balanced, or one that is not.

I first realised back in the eighties that the 'health food' pundits had got it all wrong – making us feel guilty for touching a slice of white bread or a piece of red meat, and putting us off so-called 'healthy eating' forever with diets restricted to a limited number of hard-to-chew and even-harder-to-digest items. Thus, totally unnecessarily, healthy eating, in most people's minds, became equated with torture of the worst kind!

So, about seven years ago, when I was working as part-time editor of *Slimmer* magazine, I began a campaign – through the media and my own books, and in *Slimmer* – to show that we can eat a healthy diet (well within all the current official recommendations) by adopting a much more moderate and *appealing* approach. Several years, books, TV and radio shows, videos and articles later, I know that my approach is the right one. And at last the word is getting through!

In this cookery book you will find no extremes of advice. What I say is let's eat healthily and well, and let's enjoy our food. I believe it is possible to do *both* at the same time! Over the years I have become more and more interested in cooking recipes that fit my philosophy. I have spent hours poring over the nutritionists' bible, *The Composition of Foods*, checking the nutrient content of every ingredient in every recipe. And I have proved that you can eat well on a varied diet that includes *every* type of food. Thousands of readers who have followed my diet plans and used my recipes, and are now slimmer and healthier, are the proof.

My methods, my recipes and my menus help you to cut down to the right levels of fat, sugar, salt, and so on, while getting enough of items like fibre, protein, vitamins, minerals and 'protective' foods (such as anti-oxidants).

This book contains my top one hundred very favourite healthy-eating recipes from all around the world. I've adapted many old favourites, such as coq au vin and moussaka, and I've included many new recipes. All are easy to cook, high on taste and bursting with nutritional goodness. I've achieved this by:

◆ cutting out all unnecessary fat (particularly saturated fat), but I've kept in that which is necessary for good health and for the success of the finished dish;

◆ altering the balance of food on your plate so that, by including more of certain items and less of others, the overall balance becomes healthier;

◆ adding masses of flavour, mouth-appeal and colour by using a wide range of herbs and spices, and other flavourings and ingredients;

◆ not using any low-fat, low-sugar, or other type of 'substitute' ingredient unless it works as well in a recipe as the original;

◆ buying 'lean' meats and using good-quality non-stick cooking pans, which will give excellent results with less fat.

I hope that you will cook as many of my recipes as possible, but don't forget that this is more than just a cookery book. In the first chapter you will find all the practical information and background you need to build a healthy diet, plus some set eating plans for you to follow if you like. My long-term aim is to get everyone eating in such a balanced way that they don't put on weight in the first place, but, for now, if you *do* need to lose weight, the chapter on slimming (page 19) tells you all you need to know, and provides three delicious slimming plans for you to choose from.

Within the recipe chapters there is yet more information on healthy eating. The chapter introductions include ideas and tips, plus calorie and fat counts, and the nutrition panels with each recipe (explained in chapter one) help you balance your day's menus.

Remember that the only *really* healthy diet is the one that you will stick to – and that means you need to enjoy it. The recipes in this book are *your* sort of food. And eating is *twice* as nice when it comes with no guilt attached!

Have fun . . .

CHAPTER 1

HEALTHY EATING MADE SIMPLE

Planning a healthy yet interesting diet for yourself isn't difficult, but first, of course, you need to know just what a healthy diet is. In this chapter, you'll find simple guidelines to help you choose the ideal diet. To get you off to a good start, I've also devised three weekly eating plans based on my recipes.

What is Healthy Eating?

It certainly is *not just* about fat-cutting. A healthy diet is one that is well balanced, containing enough of all the nutrients your body needs for good health and efficient operation. It should also contain the right amount of energy (calories) to maintain a reasonable body weight; it should contain not too many of the things known in excess to have a negative effect on your health; and it should include enough of the foods now thought to have a protective effect.

Let's look at these points one by one.

1 A healthy diet includes enough of all the nutrients your body needs

Everything we eat and drink consists of one or more of the following elements: fat, carbohydrate, protein, water, fibre, alcohol and trace elements, including vitamins and minerals. The right balance of all these components is the starting point for a healthy diet.

FAT is present in very many foods – and there are three main types of fat: saturated, found in largest quantity in dairy and animal produce; mono-unsaturated, found in largest quantity in olive, groundnut and rapeseed oils; and polyunsaturated, found in largest quantity in corn, sunflower, soya bean and safflower oils. All foods that contain fat contain these three types of fat in varying proportions, and perhaps trans fatty acids (see section 3, below).

All types of fat are high in calories – 9 calories per gram – and, even if we think we aren't eating a lot of fat, for most of us, 40 per cent of the calories provided by our current diet will come from fat. The health authorities throughout the Western world agree that this percentage is too high and that we should try to cut down on fat so that no more than 30 per cent of our diet is fat. (See section 3, below, for more information.) To achieve this we need to cut down on high-fat foods, such as fats and oils, cream, mayonnaise, pastry, foods fried in oil, full-fat dairy produce (such as Cheddar cheese), fatty meats, cakes, biscuits and many desserts.

CARBOHYDRATES are all the starches and sugars. For good health we should consume as much carbohydrate as possible in its natural, or near-natural, state – e.g. whole grain bread, rice, pasta, cereals, potatoes, fruit and vegetables – rather than in the form of refined sugar. We currently eat about 20 per cent of our calories in the form of sugar and approximately 24 per cent as starch. A healthier balance would be no more than 10 per cent sugars and 40–45 per cent starches, giving a total carbohydrate intake of at least 50 per cent (55 per cent would be even better). In other words, if we cut down on fat, we should replace those calories with more starchy foods.

PROTEIN is needed for cell building and repair, and we need around 10–15 per cent of our daily calories in the form of protein. Most of us get at least that amount in our daily diets, so the main thing to remember is to choose protein foods that are low in fat, most of the time. If you choose high-fat protein foods, then have smaller portions and make up the difference with extra starch.

Low-fat protein foods include: low-fat dairy produce, like skimmed milk and cottage cheese; white fish, extra-lean meat and poultry (skin removed); pulses, such as baked beans and cannellini beans, lentils and split peas; tofu and Quorn.

High-fat protein foods include: other dairy produce, like full-fat milk, Cheddar cheese, cream cheese and Stilton; fatty meat.

WATER is present in most foods and is calorie-free, with a few trace elements. We should all drink plenty of water – 2.3 litres (4 pints) a day is ideal – not only to maintain body fluid levels but also to aid digestion and to keep your kidneys and bowels in good working order.

FIBRE *see under* 'protective factors', section 4, below.

VITAMINS AND MINERALS are the trace elements we need to help our bodies work properly in very many ways. Luckily, if we are eating foods that give us a good balance of fats, carbohydrates and proteins, as discussed above, it is highly unlikely that

we will go short of these vitamins and minerals. However, it is also important to eat a wide variety of different foods within each group. For example, don't always eat just low-fat cheese and no other low-fat protein foods; cheese is a good source of calcium, but contains hardly any iron.

Here is a short list of the best sources of all the main vitamins and minerals.

Vitamin A: liver, cod liver oil, carrots, butter, green leafy veg, sweet potatoes, dried apricots, broccoli, cheese, egg yolk, low-fat spread

Vitamin D: cod liver oil, oily fish, low-fat spread, tuna, egg yolk, liver

B group vitamins: whole grains, wholemeal bread, red meat, seeds, pulses, yeast extract (e.g. Marmite), green leafy veg, nuts (Note that vitamin B_{12} is only found naturally in animal products, especially liver, kidneys, oily fish and egg yolk.)

Vitamin E: wheat germ, sunflower and safflower oil, palm oil, polyunsturated margarines, nuts, avocado, sweet potatoes, asparagus, salmon, whole meal flour or bread, brown rice

Vitamin C: most fresh fruit and vegetables, especially red pepper, blackcurrants, parsley, broccoli, green peppers, citrus fruits, strawberries, cabbage and leafy greens, mango, potato, peas, pineapple, tomatoes

Calcium (Ca): seaweed, Parmesan cheese, Cheddar, Edam, sardines, tofu, other cheeses, nuts, yogurt, haricot beans, leafy greens, prawns, other pulses, milk, egg yolk, muesli

Magnesium (Mg): cocoa powder, wheat bran, wheat germ, nuts, pulses, oats, brown rice, dried fruits, bananas, potatoes

Iron (Fe): liver, red meat, dark green vegetables, curry powder, pulses, dried apricots, wholemeal bread, bulghar, couscous, eggs

Zinc (Zn): oysters, wheat germ, wheat bran, liver, sunflower seeds, oats, beef, nuts, cheese, shellfish, pulses, brown rice, wholemeal bread, sweetcorn

Potassium (K): seaweed, dried apricots, pulses, dates, nuts, potatoes, mushrooms, oily fish, coconut, pasta, avocado, pork, sweet potato, bananas, beef, lamb, broccoli, peas

2 A healthy diet provides the right amount of energy (calories) to maintain a reasonable body weight

If you eat too many calories for your own needs, you will put on weight. If you eat too few, you will lose weight. People differ in their calorie requirements – active people need many more calories a day than inactive people, for instance, and as we get older we need fewer calories.

   To maintain a healthy weight, most women need around 1900 calories and men 2500 calories, but these amounts are only a guide. If you need to lose weight, read the next chapter.

3 A healthy diet does not include too many of the things known to have a possible negative effect on your health

SATURATED FATS When cutting your fat intake to bring it into line with the recommended intake of 30 per cent of daily calories, it's wise first to cut down on the saturated fats in your diet because saturated fat is the fat linked with heart and circulatory disease. It is now also thought that *trans fatty acids* (found in many commercial products, such as hard and some other margarines, biscuits and other baked goods) have a similar effect to saturated fats, so it's wise also to cut down on these.

SUGAR There's no harm at all in a small amount of sugar in your diet, especially if you are underweight or of average weight. But it is wise to limit the amount of sugar you eat, not only because sugar contains no nutrients at all, except calories, but also because snacking on sugary foods, or replacing 'real' meals with sugary items, can lead to excessive fluctuations in your blood sugar levels.

SODIUM Salt is a mixture of 40 per cent sodium and 60 per cent chloride. A high sodium intake in susceptible people is related to high blood pressure. Department of Health guidelines suggest that we should try to limit our daily sodium intake to no more than 1600 mg a day, which represents less than a teaspoonful of salt. If you've been advised by your doctor to follow a low-salt diet, you can use a salt substitute in the recipes, where appropriate, although I have kept added-salt and high-salt foods to a minimum. Unless otherwise stated, the quantity of salt used in a recipe is ⅓ teaspoon maximum (or less, to taste).

4 A healthy diet includes plenty of the protective factors that may help prevent disease and/or improve health

UNSATURATED OILS When reducing the overall amount of fat in your diet, it is best not to reduce the amount of *mono-unsaturates* and *polyunsaturates* too much because they do have a positive effect on your body. Polyunsaturates and mono-unsaturates offer protection against heart disease by reducing levels in the blood of the type of cholesterol that blocks the arteries. Certain polyunsaturates may also help prevent or treat osteoporosis. And the polyunsaturates found in oily fish – 'omega-3s' – help prevent heart disease and strokes by reducing the risk of blood clots.

ANTI-OXIDANTS In the war against heart disease and cancer, the latest allies are the anti-oxidant vitamins, beta-carotene (which converts to vitamin A in our bodies), vitamin C and vitamin E. Numerous trials have shown that a high intake of these anti-oxidants is linked with a reduced risk of heart disease and various types of cancer. A list of high vitamin C and E foods appears in section 1, above. The best sources of beta-carotene are all the orange- and yellow-fleshed fruits and vegetables, and dark green vegetables. Luckily, these are also all good sources of vitamin C.

FIBRE The starchy carbohydrate foods – 'complex' carbohydrates such as whole grain cereals, rice, pasta, bread, potatoes, pulses, fruits and vegetables – are our main sources of fibre in the diet. There are two types of fibre – *insoluble* (such as that found in bran), which helps keep you 'regular', and *soluble* (such as that found in pulses, oats and fruit), which also offers protection against heart disease by lowering blood cholesterol. So it is important to include high soluble-fibre foods in your healthy diet as well as high insoluble-fibre foods. We should aim for 18 g fibre a day. A diet high in complex carbohydrates also seems to offer protection against some forms of cancer.

GARLIC If you like garlic, it's worth including plenty in your diet as it is a powerful antiseptic and may also help reduce blood clotting and high blood pressure.

WINE Wine may offer protection against heart disease, too, so don't feel guilty for indulging in a glass or two a day!

DAILY FAT INTAKE

Below is a quick guide to how many grams of fat you should be eating a day to give you a maximum of 30 per cent of daily calories in the form of fat. Only a third of your 'fat' calories should be saturated fat.

	Total fat	Saturated fat
Women on 1900 calories a day	63 g	21 g
Men on 2500 calories a day	83 g	27 g

As the fat content of all the recipes in this book, and all the calorie-counted items listed, is given, it's easy occasionally to check and see whether, indeed, you are managing to cut your fat levels down to roughly these amounts. Remember – first cut your saturated fats.

The Recipes

All the recipes in this book serve four, except the ice cream desserts. If you are serving fewer people, you can easily reduce the ingredients quantities accordingly, or portions of many recipes can be frozen for another time.

When planning a healthy diet of your own, bear in mind the information in this chapter.

This information, and the nutrition panels that accompany the recipes, will help you balance your diet.

THE NUTRITION PANELS

Calorie and fat counts are self-explanatory. Bear in mind that on a weight maintenance diet you are aiming for around 1900 calories a day in total for women and 2500 for men; and that you are aiming for no more than 63 g total fat (21 g saturated fat) a day for women and 83 g total fat (27 g saturated fat) a day for men.

Protein content is star rated. ★ means the dish contains under 10 per cent of its calories as protein; ★★ means the dish contains between 10 per cent and 15 per cent; and ★★★ means it contains over 15 per cent.

Fibre content is star rated. ★ means the dish contains less than 2 g of fibre per portion; ★★ means it contains between 2 g and 6 g fibre per portion; and ★★★ means it contains over 6 g fibre per portion.

Carbohydrate content is star rated. ★ means the dish contains under 35 per cent carbohydrate; ★★ means it contains between 35 per cent and 50 per cent carbohydrate; and ★★★ means it contains over 50 per cent carbohydrate per portion.

Vitamins and minerals mentioned are those found in significant quantities in the dish, starting with the greatest. Other unlisted vitamins and minerals may be present in smaller amounts.

Special notes appear on some recipes for people on low-salt or low-cholesterol diets, if the recipe contains more than 1000 mg salt or 90 mg cholesterol.

ACHIEVING A BALANCE

When choosing a recipe, you might think it doesn't appear to contain enough carbohydrate or fibre (for example) to be healthy, or that perhaps it contains more fat than is ideal. However, when you consider what is to be served with that dish you will almost always find that the balance does become healthy. For example, French Provincial Soup with Red Pesto (page 30) is high in protein and fibre but contains less than that ideal 50 per cent-plus of carbohydrate. If you serve it with the good portion of bread suggested, however, the total protein content of the meal goes down and the total carbohydrate content goes up. As another example, Spicy Red Kebabs with Tomato Sauce (page 54) contains only medium amounts of fibre and is low in carbohydrate. However, when served with rice and salad, the meal contains more fibre and would be rated ★★★ for carbohydrate.

Also bear in mind that you should balance out your meals throughout the day. For instance, after a very low-fat lunch, such as Watercress and Potato Soup (page 31), you could happily indulge yourself a little more in the evening with, for instance, Moussaka (page 55).

If you want to know what percentage of fat you are eating in any recipe, multiply the grams of fat in a portion by nine (because each gram of fat contains 9 calories), and then work that figure out as a percentage of the total calories per portion in the dish. For example, Real Chilli con Carne (page 45) contains 9 g fat per portion. That is 81 calories, which is 19.28 per cent of the total calories per portion (420). My chilli, then, is much lower in fat than the 30 per cent of total calories that your daily fat content should ideally be.

You see, healthy, reduced-fat eating *is* all about balance. Get that balance right and you need never pile on the pounds again. However, if it's too late and you already need to lose some weight, turn to page 19.

Using the Eating Plans

I have drawn up two weekly plans, using some of the recipes in this book, but including other meal suggestions as well. Each plan provides you with a balanced diet – nutrient content varies from day to day, but over the week works out at the right levels. In the plans, detailed on pages 14–17, recipes for all the dishes in *italics* can be found in later chapters of this book.

You don't have to follow one of my plans at all, of course – you may prefer to devise your own healthy diet using the recipes and information throughout the book. But if you do decide to follow a plan, please read the following information first.

MEN, and some other people (such as hungry teenagers), may need to eat more and they should have either bigger portions or extra carbohydrates and milk.

PORTION SIZES in the plans are only a guide.

LUNCHES Most lunches can be packed and taken to work or school if you have suitable containers, such as a wide-necked flask for soup and an insulated container for salads. Taking your own packed lunch to work is usually a healthier option than buying a take-away lunch.

RECIPES When a recipe is mentioned within a plan, it is assumed that you will eat a quarter, as all recipes are designed to serve four. All non-recipe meals in the plans serve one.

DRINKS You have a milk allowance for tea and coffee, or to drink on its own. You can also have drinks from the 'Unlimiteds' list below, and alcohol appears in the optional 'Extras' lists.

BREAD, RICE AND PASTA Try to choose whole grain bread, brown rice and wholewheat pasta at least some of the time, where the type isn't specified in the plan, as the whole grain versions provide extra fibre, vitamins and minerals. But there is nothing wrong with white bread some of the time – it is a good source of calcium.

UNLIMITEDS The following foods and drinks can be included in unlimited quantities in your healthy eating plan, and you should make full use of them. Remember particularly to have lots of salad items and enough water.

Drinks Water, mineral water, tea and coffee (sugar only if choosing from 'Extras'), herbal teas, low-calorie squashes and diet drinks (but try not to rely on these too much)

Eats Any leafy salad greens, spring onions, cucumber, pickled onions, oil-free French dressing, all fresh or dried herbs and spices, garlic, lemon juice, lime juice, chilli sauce, mustard, soy sauce, Worcestershire sauce, tomato purée, artificial sweeteners

EXTRAS Each plan allows you a certain number of 'extras' which you can choose from the following lists. However, you should try to limit your 'Extras' fat grams to no more than 15 g a day (so, for example, your maximum butter allowance on any day would be two 50-calorie portions, giving you 12 g of fat). On the slimming plans in chapter 2 you should limit yourself to no more than 7 g 'Extras' fat in any one day. (In these lists, those dishes marked with an asterisk can be found in this book.)

EXTRAS

50-calorie Extras	Fat (grams)
1 piece fruit (apple, orange, pear, peach, nectarine)	trace
large serving berry fruits	trace
2 Sunblest Crisprolls	2
2 rye crispbreads	0.4
1 reduced-fat Digestive biscuit	2.0
heaped teaspoon butter (7 g)	6.0
2 teaspoons low-fat spread (12 g)	5.0
1 tablespoon reduced-fat mayonnaise	4.5
1 rye crispbread with 1 tablespoon Shape cheese spread	1.75
50 g (2 oz) plain boiled potato	trace
2 rounded tablespoons cooked rice	trace
3 tablespoons low-fat custard	1.0
25 ml (1 fl oz) half-fat crème fraîche or half-fat cream	4.0
1 Shape diet fruit yogurt	0.1
1 Shape diet fromage frais (100 g/3½ oz)	0.1
2 teaspoons sugar or honey	nil
1 Jaffa cake	1.0

100-calorie Extras	Fat (grams)
1 banana or mango	0.3
shades of Red Fruit Salad*	0.25
Medium slice of bread, low-fat spread and low-sugar jam	2.5
Carrot and Tomato Soup*	6.0
15 g (½ oz) butter	12.0

100-calorie Extras	Fat (grams)
100 g (3½ oz) potato	trace
1 chunk roast potato	4.5
1 tablespoon peanut butter	9.0
2 teaspoons mayonnaise (full fat)	8.0
1 tablespoon French dressing	11.0
15 g (½ oz) slice of malt loaf	0.4
125 ml (4½ fl oz) WeightWatchers ice cream	3.5
tube of Polo mints	0.3
1 Lo or Halo chocolate bar	4.7/3.8
20 g (¾ oz) bar Cadbury's Dairy Milk	6.0
Kit Kat (2 fingers)	5.7
140 ml (5 fl oz) glass dry or medium dry wine	nil
275 ml (½ pint) cider, beer or lager	nil
1 double measure any spirit	nil

250-calorie Extras	Fat (grams)
any starter or dessert in this book at 250 calories or less per portion	varies, check nutrition panels
75 g (3 oz) baguette	2.6
½ bottle dry or medium dry wine	nil
3 cream crackers with 40 g (1½ oz) Cheddar cheese	15.0
sandwich of 2 medium slices bread with low-fat spread and 50 g (2 oz) chicken or 1 hard-boiled egg or 100 g (3½ oz) crabmeat or tuna	9.5

THE FAMILY PLAN

This is the ideal plan for people who have to cook for a family – with an eye on the budget, too.

About 1900 calories a day

Every day In addition to the meals listed, each person should have a daily allowance of 275 ml (½ pint) skimmed or 175 ml (6½ fl oz) semi-skimmed milk. (Children of 5 years and under should have full-cream milk.) Each person can also have every day any item(s) from the 'Extras' list on page 13 up to a maximum of 250 calories. Eat 'Unlimited' items (see page 13) as you like.

RECIPES

Calorie- and fat-counted recipes for all the dishes in italics can be found in later chapters of this book – see the index for page numbers.

DAY 1

BREAKFAST

125 g (4½ oz) carton of low-fat natural Bio yogurt with 1 medium banana chopped in

1 average slice of wholemeal bread with a little low-fat spread and 1 teaspoon pure fruit spread or Marmite

LUNCH

Lentil and Bacon Soup
granary bap
1 satsuma or similar

EVENING MEAL

Chicken Paprika
50 g (2 oz) ribbon noodles, (tagliatelle or fettucine), boiled
green salad or spring greens (large portion)
2 scoops *Raspberry Ice*

DAY 2

BREAKFAST

medium bowl of oat bran flakes or Shreddies with skimmed milk to cover (extra to allowance) and 1 apple chopped in

1 medium glass of orange juice

LUNCH

1 large baked potato (with a little butter counted as an 'extra', if liked – see list)

grated carrot mixed with 25 g (1 oz) grated Edam cheese
100 g (3½ oz) low-fat Greek yogurt (e.g. Total), mixed with 2 teaspoons runny honey and 1 tablespoon sultanas

EVENING MEAL

Baked Pasta with Smoked Haddock and Peas
broccoli
Bananas Suzette

DAY 3

BREAKFAST

average serving (about 8 pieces) of mixed dried fruit (prunes, apricots, peaches, apples, pears), simmered in water until tender and served with some of the cooking juices 125 g (4½ oz) carton of low-fat natural Bio yogurt

small slice of bread with a little low-fat spread and pure fruit spread

LUNCH

1 wholemeal pitta bread filled with 50 g (2 oz) feta cheese, crumbled and mixed with chopped cucumber, tomato, onion and unlimited salad (see page 120) of your choice, all tossed in oil-free French dressing plus 1 dessertspoon olive oil

1 orange or nectarine

EVENING MEAL

Real Chilli con Carne and Rice
green salad with oil-free French dressing
sliced cantaloupe melon or peaches with 100 g (3½ oz) 8 per cent fat fromage frais

DAY 4

BREAKFAST
As Day Two but with orange instead of apple

LUNCH
Pasta, Bacon and Apple Crunch
1 large slice of wholemeal bread with a little
low-fat spread

EVENING
English Cod and Prawn Pie
average serving of sweetcorn, peas and carrots
average serving of grapes and 1 scoop reduced-
calorie vanilla ice cream

DAY 5

BREAKFAST
As Day One

LUNCH
Large granary bap filled with 100 g (3½ oz)
canned tuna in brine, drained, plus 2 tablespoons
drained canned butter beans, and unlimited salad
items, plus sliced tomato

1 dessertspoon 70 per cent fat-free mayonnaise
handful of ready-to-eat dried apricots

EVENING MEAL
Cheese, Potato and Pepper Pie
average portion of spinach
Saint Clement's Pancakes with 1 tablespoon
half-fat crème fraîche

DAY 6

BREAKFAST
50 g (2 oz) no-added-sugar muesli with
skimmed milk to cover

1 medium glass of orange juice

LUNCH
Watercress and Potato Soup★
75 g (3 oz) French bread
1 medium banana and a handful of ready-to-eat
dried apricots or peaches

EVENING MEAL
Classic Lasagne
mixed leaf salad with oil-free French dressing
Strawberry and Peach Layer

DAY 7

BREAKFAST
1 size-3 egg, poached

1 large slice of wholemeal toast with a little
low-fat spread

1 medium glass of orange juice

LUNCH
50 g (2 oz) hummus (ready-made or home-
made) with a selection of crudités and 1 pitta
bread, sliced

2 pieces of fresh fruit of choice

EVENING MEAL
Provençal Baked Chicken and Vegetables
1 medium (225 g/8 oz) baked potato
Apricot and Nut Crumble
100 ml (3½ fl oz) low-fat custard

THE DEMI-VEGETARIAN PLAN

If you enjoy a predominantly vegetarian diet, but do like to eat fish, or perhaps a little chicken, occasionally, here's the plan for you.

About 1900 calories a day

Every day You have a 275 ml (½ pint) allowance of skimmed milk and 250 calories' worth of 'Extras' from the items listed on page 13, plus 'Unlimiteds' as listed (page 13).

RECIPES

Calorie- and fat-counted recipes for all the dishes in italics can be found in later chapters of this book – see the index for page numbers.

DAY 1

BREAKFAST
average serving (about 8 pieces) of mixed dried fruit (prunes, apricots, peaches, apples, pears), simmered in water until tender and served with some of the cooking juices

125 g (4½ oz) carton of low-fat natural Bio yogurt

small slice of bread with a little low-fat spread and pure fruit spread

LUNCH
Prawn, Rice and Avocado Salad
1 slice of wholemeal bread from a large loaf with a little low-fat spread

1 orange

EVENING MEAL
Fusilli Napoletana
large mixed salad with oil-free French dressing
Brown Bread Ice Cream with Apricot Sauce

DAY 2

BREAKFAST
2 Weetabix with skimmed milk to cover
1 large banana

LUNCH
French Provincial Soup with Tomato Pesto
60 g (2½ oz) portion of French bread
1 kiwi fruit or satsuma

EVENING
Salmon Skewers with Hot Sauce and Avocado
Easy Summer Pudding with 2 tablespoons half-fat cream

DAY 3

BREAKFAST
50 g (2 oz) no-added-sugar muesli with skimmed milk to cover

1 orange, peach or nectarine

LUNCH
Waldorf Salad in Pasta Shells
1 diet fruit fromage frais (100 g/3½ oz)

EVENING
Carrot and Tomato Soup
1 slice of wholemeal bread from a large loaf
Chilli Rice and Chickpeas
Apricot and Nut Crumble

DAY 4

BREAKFAST
As Day One

LUNCH
1 slice of rye or wholemeal bread from a large loaf (or 2 small slices to make a sandwich)

50 g (2 oz) gravadlax *or* 100 g (3½ oz) canned tuna in brine, drained cucumber and mixed leaf salad

mixed fresh fruit salad (home-made or bought, chilled)

100 g (3½ oz) low-fat Greek yogurt

EVENING MEAL
Best-Ever Vegetable Lasagne
green salad
Bananas Suzette

DAY 5

BREAKFAST
As Day Two

LUNCH
half a 225 g (8 oz) can of mixed bean salad, drained and mixed with 150 g (5½ oz) cooked brown rice, French dressing, 50 g (2 oz) chopped cooked chicken or canned pink salmon, sliced raw button mushrooms and chopped lettuce (cos, iceberg or Chinese leaves)

1 apple and 100 ml (3½ fl oz) 8 per cent fat fromage frais

EVENING MEAL
Cheese, Potato and Pepper Pie
mixed salad
Exotic Fruits Brûlée

DAY 6

BREAKFAST
125 g (4½ oz) carton of low-fat natural Bio yogurt mixed with 4 ready-to-eat dried apricots, chopped, and 1 chopped apple

25 g (1 oz) slice of bread with a little low-fat spread and 1 teaspoon honey or pure fruit spread

LUNCH
Grilled Halloumi and Aubergine with Pitta
1 large banana

EVENING MEAL
Mixed Paella, made with firm white fish instead of chicken if you don't eat chicken

large mixed side salad
Braised Peaches with Strawberry Fool

DAY 7

BREAKFAST
1 large egg, boiled or poached
1 large slice of wholemeal bread with a little low-fat spread

1 large orange or 2 satsumas

LUNCH
Onion Bruschetta (double serving)

EVENING MEAL
Catalan Tuna Casserole
granary bread roll
Shades of Red Fruit Salad
2 tablespoons half-fat crème fraîche or Greek yogurt

DINNER-PARTY MENU PLANNERS

This section provides a selection of three-course dinner-party menus using the recipes in this book. Each has its own international theme and is designed to provide an attractive, balanced meal that will please your guests but not leave them with that leaden, after-dinner feeling that an over-rich menu can bring. Recipes for those dishes in italics can be found in the following chapters of this book.

FRENCH

Salade Maison

....

French Country Chicken Casserole
New potatoes
Selection of vegetables

....

Bananas Suzette
Half-fat crème fraîche

BRITISH

Smoked Trout Pâté
Toast

....

Venison and Mushroom Casserole
Olive-oil mashed potato
Selection of vegetables

....

*Brown Bread Ice Cream with
Apricot Sauce*

VEGETARIAN

Garlic Mushrooms
French bread

....

*Mixed Vegetables with a
Spicy Stuffing*
Selection of side salads

....

Exotic Fruits Brûlée

MEXICAN

Guacamole
Tortilla chips and crudités

....

Sizzling Beef Fajitas with Salsa

....

Raspberry Ice

MEDITERRANEAN

*Tomatoes Stuffed with Pesto and
Mozzarella*

....

Spanish Chicken
Green leaf and herb salad

....

Shades of Red Fruit Salad

CHAPTER 2

SLIMMING MADE SIMPLE

If you need to lose some weight, you *can* do it without endless misery, or having to live on a diet of limp lettuce and minuscule portions. On pages 22 to 27 are three slimming plans for you to choose from, based around recipes in this book. Whichever one you decide to try, I can assure you that you'll be very pleasantly surprised at both the amount you can eat and the good tastes you will savour. But first I'd like to give you some tips on healthy slimming and some more ideas on how to make your diet enjoyable.

Before you do anything else, read the first chapter in this book; it will give you all the background knowledge you need on healthy eating. Next, work out your Body Mass Index (BMI) to see if you really do need to lose weight. Find your calculator and follow these simple steps:

1. Write down your current weight in kilograms. (If you need to convert pounds into kilos, just divide the pounds by 2.2.)

2. Write down your height in metres. (If you need to convert inches into metres, multiply by 0.025.)

3. 'Square' your height (e.g. if you are 1.6 metres tall, multiply 1.6 by 1.6 to discover your 'squared' height of 2.56).

4. Divide your weight (in kilos) by your squared height. The result is your Body Mass Index. Here's what it means:

Below 20	Underweight
20–25	Acceptable weight
25–30	Becoming overweight
30–40	Obese
Over 40	Very obese

If your BMI is 30 or over, you definitely need to lose some weight; if it is 25 or under you don't.

But if you are in that 'grey area' between 25 and 30 – especially if you are over 40 or your surplus weight is mostly around your hips and thighs – you may not need to lose any weight. (Surplus weight carried around the waist and tummy is more of a health risk than the 'pear shape'.) And if you are at the lower end of the 25–30 bracket, there is less need to worry about your weight than if you are getting near the 30 mark.

If you decide that you *do* need to shed some fat, you can either pick one of the plans that follow (which is what I'd recommend you do, at least to start with) or you can devise your own diet using the recipes and other foods of your own choice.

Cutting calories

The only diet that will help you lose weight is one that reduces the number of calories you eat to a sufficiently low level to make your body burn up its own surplus fat for energy.

To do this safely you need to lose weight slowly,

so that you don't go short of nutrients. First and foremost you need to cut down on the fat you eat, particularly the saturated fat (see page 10). This is also the easiest way to reduce your calorie intake as fat contains more than twice as many calories per gram than either protein or carbohydrate.

The good thing about slimming by cutting down your fat intake is that you don't necessarily have to count the calories in all your food in order to lose weight. As long as you keep a careful eye on the amount of fat you eat, all research shows that you *will* lose weight steadily while eating your fill of carbohydrates (and protein). That's because a low-fat diet naturally and effortlessly reduces your overall calorie intake to a slimming level.

In the first chapter, I said that a healthy fat intake is no more than 30 per cent of total calories. When you're slimming, you need to cut the fat even further. Thirty per cent of a 1900-calories-a-day weight maintenance diet is 570 calories, which is equivalent to 63 g of fat. Cut the fat to 30 g a day (an acceptable level as long as it is mostly saturated fat you are cutting) and you save 300 (33 × 9) calories a day, but you won't feel hungry because you will still be eating as much carbohydrate as you were before.

Just by cutting 33 g fat you will be saving 2100 calories a week which, on its own, would produce a weight-loss of over half a pound (0.2 kg) a week or about two stone (12.7 kg) in a year! If you then just cut down very slightly on your carbohydrates and protein – say, eat 11 g less of protein a day and 60 g less of carbohydrate a day (preferably by reducing the sugars, not the starches), you will still be getting plenty on your plate but you'll save another 288 calories a day and then lose over a pound (0.5 kg) a week.

You don't need or want to lose weight any faster than that because we now know that it could be dangerous – although in the first week or two of any diet you will lose more weight because you are shedding body fluids as well as fat. But after the end of week two, two pounds a week (or less) is ideal.

My slimming plans are low-fat plans based on around 1300 calories a day with a 20 per cent fat content. If you are more than a stone (6.4 kg) or so

overweight (or with a BMI of more than 30, or male, or a teenager), it is wise to add extra carbohydrate (bread, potatoes, pasta or rice) to this basic plan (up to 200 extra calories) at least for the first few weeks of slimming. This will stop you from feeling hungry and ensure you don't lose weight too fast.

Practicalities

Here are some practical ways to help you cut your fat intake (particularly your saturated fat intake:

◆ Buy as many low-fat and reduced-fat versions of higher-fat foods as you can (e.g. low-fat yogurt, oil-free French dressing).

◆ Cook with no fat or with as little as possible, and if you do use an unsaturated oil.

◆ Buy extra-lean cuts of meat and grill any meat where fat will melt and pour out (e.g. bacon).

◆ Look upon high-fat items, like pastries, biscuits, cake and cream, as occasional treats rather than regular fixtures in your diet. If building your own diet, use the 'Extras' lists on page 13 to allow yourself a little treat now and then.

◆ Replace fatty ingredients (such as butter and cream) with tasty low-fat ingredients (such as herbs, spices, juices, vinegars and passata).

Motivational Tips

◆ Remember to keep as much variety in your diet as possible.

◆ Don't skip meals or try to slim on less than 1300 calories a day.

◆ Take plenty of exercise to help burn off the fat.

◆ Plan your week's eating and shopping so that you aren't caught with nothing suitable in the fridge to eat when you are hungry.

◆ Between meals, snack on fruit or crudités.

◆ Keep hunger at bay by having plenty of carbo-hydrate at every meal (bread, potatoes, pasta, rice, cereal, pulses), but don't eat more than you need to satisfy hunger.

◆ Have plenty of high-fibre foods – beans and lentils, dried fruits such as prunes and apricots, whole grain cereals and vegetables.

◆ Make dishes look appealing.

◆ Eat slowly and chew your food thoroughly.

◆ Drink plenty (preferably water) with your meal.

And lastly . . .

I am sure that you will succeed in losing your surplus pounds this time. Once you've lost enough pounds to bring your BMI down to a reasonable level (do the BMI test again with your new weight every now and again if you are not sure), the most important thing of all is to keep the weight off. For that, keep practising everything you've learnt about a healthy diet – and, most of all, enjoy your food and your cooking!

QUICK AND EASY SLIMMING PLAN

If you haven't a lot of time to spare, you can still shape up with this plan. All your meals are quick to prepare, and easy too. Ingredients for the recipes can be scaled down to suit one or two people.

About 1300 calories a day

Every day You have a skimmed milk allowance of 140 ml (¼ pint), and you can choose 100 calories' worth of 'Extras' from the list on page 13, plus 'Unlimited' items from page 13. All milk mentioned below is in addition to your allowance.

APRICOT PILAU

If you make this rice dish (recipe on page 116), you can freeze the surplus. Alternatively, buy some ready-made pilau from the delicatessen or chill counter of your local supermarket and serve yourself 5 tablespoons.

DAY 2

BREAKFAST
125 g (4½ oz) carton low-fat natural Bio yogurt with 5 chopped ready-to-eat dried apricots and 1 piece fresh fruit of choice

LUNCH
2 medium slices of wholemeal bread filled with 100 g (3½ oz) drained canned tuna in brine, a few drained canned butter beans, slices of tomato and spring onion, plus 2 teaspoons 70 per cent fat-free mayonnaise

1 banana

EVENING MEAL
Aromatic Turkey with Citrus Sauce
Apricot Pilau (see box)
green salad

DAY 1

BREAKFAST
average serving of Bran Flakes with skimmed milk to cover

1 satsuma

LUNCH
Pasta, Bacon and Apple Crunch

EVENING MEAL
Tandoori Cod Bake
average serving of boiled basmati or quick-cook long-grain white rice
mixed salad

1 mango

DAY 3

BREAKFAST
1 medium slice of wholemeal bread with a little low-fat spread and pure fruit spread

1 orange

LUNCH
Carrot and Tomato Soup
Average granary roll

125 g (4½ oz) carton low-fat natural Bio yogurt
1 medium banana

EVENING MEAL
Spicy Kedgeree
mixed salad

DAY 4

BREAKFAST
25 g (1 oz) no-added-sugar muesli with
skimmed milk to cover

1 nectarine or peach

LUNCH
Guacamole
1 wholemeal pitta bread

1 large banana

EVENING
Halibut Steaks with a Crusted Herb Topping
or *Monkfish, Prawn and Red Pepper Stir-Fry*
average serving of rice noodles

125 ml (4½ fl oz) low-calorie vanilla ice cream

DAY 5

BREAKFAST
As Day One

LUNCH
60 g (2½ oz) portion of French bread with a little
low-fat spread

50 g (2 oz) half-fat Cheddar-style cheese or
extra-lean roast beef

large mixed salad with oil-free French dressing
2 teaspoons pickle
1 apple

EVENING MEAL
Spaghetti with Bacon and Pesto
green salad

DAY 6

BREAKFAST
As Day Two

LUNCH
Lentil and Bacon Soup, made without the bacon
1 medium slice of wholemeal bread

EVENING MEAL
Mixed Pepper Tortilla
50 g (2 oz) bread
green salad

DAY 7

BREAKFAST
2 Weetabix with skimmed milk to cover
½ pink grapefruit

LUNCH
200 g (7 oz) baked beans on 1 large slice of
wholemeal toast

1 orange
125 g (4½ oz) carton low-fat natural Bio yogurt

EVENING MEAL
Beef Stroganoff and Noodles
large green salad

1 slice of cantaloupe melon or serving of
strawberries

VEGETARIAN SLIMMING PLAN

Choose this plan if you don't eat meat, poultry or fish, and discover some exciting new vegetarian flavours while you lose weight!

About 1300 calories a day

Every day You have a skimmed milk allowance of 140 ml (¼ pint) and you can choose 100 calories' worth of 'Extras' from the list on page 13, as well as 'unlimited' items from page 13. Breakfast milk is in addition to your daily allowance.

RECIPES

Calorie- and fat-counted recipes for all the dishes in italics can be found in later chapters of this book – see the index for page numbers.

DAY 2

BREAKFAST

125 g (4½ oz) carton low-fat natural Bio yogurt with 25 g (1 oz) dried fruit of choice chopped in

1 apple or orange

LUNCH

50 g (2 oz) ready-made vegetable pâté or 25 g (1 oz) Tartex mushroom pâté
1 baguette or 2 petits pains
mixed salad

1 small banana

EVENING MEAL

French Provincial Soup with Tomato Pesto
1 large slice of wholemeal bread

fruit yogurt or 150 ml (5½ fl oz) low-calorie vanilla ice cream

DAY 1

BREAKFAST

1 medium slice of wholemeal bread with a little low-fat spread and pure fruit spread
1 orange

LUNCH

Onion Bruschetta

100 g (3½ oz) low-fat Greek yogurt with 2 teaspoons honey and 1 tablespoon sultanas

EVENING MEAL

Best-Ever Vegetable Lasagne
large mixed-leaf salad

DAY 3

BREAKFAST

2 Weetabix with skimmed milk to cover
½ pink grapefruit

LUNCH

Grilled Halloumi and Aubergine with Pitta

1 kiwi fruit and 1 apple

EVENING MEAL

Three-Mushroom Risotto
mixed salad

50 g (2 oz) 8 per cent fat fromage frais with portion of soft fruit of choice or grapes

DAY 4

BREAKFAST
2 medium slices of wholemeal bread with a little
low-fat spread and 2 teaspoons honey
½ grapefruit

LUNCH
Waldorf Salad in Pasta Shells

EVENING MEAL
Ratatouille and Lentil Gratin
large mixed salad
granary roll

1 medium banana

DAY 5

BREAKFAST
As Day Two

LUNCH
Watercress and Potato Soup
granary roll with low-fat spread
50 g (2 oz) medium-fat goat's cheese or feta
cheese

average portion of grapes

EVENING MEAL
Oriental Stir-Fry

1 diet fruit yogurt

DAY 6

BREAKFAST
As Day Three

LUNCH
Large bap or burger bun filled with 1 Quorn
burger *or* 1 ready-made Falafel Patty *or* 1 hard-
boiled egg, sliced, plus mixed salad

slice of cantaloupe melon *or* 2 slices of fresh
pineapple or canned pineapple in juice

EVENING MEAL
Garlic Mushrooms
40 g (1½ oz) portion of French bread
Pumpkin, Spinach and Cauliflower Bake

DAY 7

BREAKFAST
As Day One

LUNCH
50 g (2 oz) ready-made hummus (see page 18)
1 wholemeal pitta bread
mixed salad

5 ready-to-eat dried apricots

EVENING MEAL
Pasta Harlequin Bake

Pears Poached in Red Wine

THE SUIT-YOURSELF SLIMMING PLAN

Here's an ideal plan for people who prefer to stick to their slimming for five days a week, then to have two much more relaxed days at the weekend.

Days 1 to 5: about 1100 calories a day

Every day For the first five days you have a skimmed milk allowance of 140 ml (¼ pint), and you can choose 50 calories' worth of 'Extras' from the list on page 13, plus 'Unlimiteds' from page 13.

RECIPES

Calorie- and fat-counted recipes for all the dishes in italics can be found in later chapters of this book – see the index for page numbers.

DAY 1

BREAKFAST
portion of porridge, made with water and 25 g (1 oz) oats, with skimmed milk to cover

5 ready-to-eat dried apricots

LUNCH
½ medium avocado, sliced and arranged with 1 slice cantaloupe melon and 25 g (1 oz) peeled prawns; oil-free French dressing drizzled over

50 g (2 oz) bread

EVENING MEAL
Hungarian Beef Goulash
green salad

DAY 2

BREAKFAST
fresh fruit salad (2 or 3 pieces of fruit)
125 g (4½ oz) carton low-fat natural Bio yogurt

LUNCH
50 g (2 oz) medium-fat goat's cheese, grilled and served on mixed salad leaves

granary bap

EVENING MEAL
Seafood Risotto
mixed salad

DAY 3

BREAKFAST
1 Weetabix, crumbled on to 125 g (4½ oz) low-fat natural Bio yogurt, and 2 teaspoons sunflower seeds sprinkled over

LUNCH
50 g (2 oz) hummus (see page 18)
1 pitta bread

portion of grapes

EVENING MEAL
Bacon and Vegetable Gratin
mixed salad

DAY 4

BREAKFAST
40 g (1½ oz) no-added-sugar muesli with
skimmed milk to cover

½ pink grapefruit

LUNCH
75 g (3 oz) baguette filled with 1 hard-boiled
egg, sliced, 2 teaspoons 70 per cent fat-free
mayonnaise and unlimited salad

1 kiwi fruit or satsuma

EVENING MEAL
Chilli Barbecued Monkfish with Herb Couscous

DAY 5

BREAKFAST
As Day Two

LUNCH
Tuna and Artichoke Salad
1 medium slice of wholemeal bread with a little
low-fat spread

EVENING MEAL
Pork Tenderloins in Spicy Mustard Sauce
70 g (2½ oz) tagliatelle or fettuccine verde,
cooked
portion of broccoli

Days 6 and 7: about 1600 calories a day

On both days You have a milk allowance of
275 ml (½ pint) skimmed milk, or 175 ml
(6½ fl oz) semi-skimmed milk, and you can have
1 glass of dry or medium dry wine or cham-
pagne with your evening meal.

DAY 6

BREAKFAST
As Day Four

LUNCH
Curried Rice Salad with Chicken and Bananas

EVENING MEAL
Turkish Lamb Kebab Pittas or *Beef Stroganoff and
Noodles*
green salad

Braised Peaches with Strawberry Fool

DAY 7

BREAKFAST
As Day One

LUNCH
French Provincial Soup with Red Pesto
1 granary roll

EVENING MEAL
Salmon and Broccoli Pancakes
average portion of peas
mixed salad
or
Garlic Chicken Roast
175 g (6 oz) new potatoes, scrubbed, brushed
with olive oil and roasted
pumpkin chunks brushed with olive oil and
roasted
average portion of spinach

Easy Summer Pudding with 2 tablespoons
half-fat cream

CHAPTER 3

SOUPS, SNACKS AND STARTERS

Here is a collection of some of my favourite 'little meals', not all of which need be used as starters. Indeed, some are much too filling to begin a meal, but make ideal light lunches or suppers. Alternatively, choose two recipes from this chapter to make a complete meal.

Many of the other dishes in this book will also make good starters and snacks if quantities are reduced. For example, half portions of most of the salads (pages 120–131) would be ideal. Here are some more ideas:

Salmon Fishcakes (page 79) – halve the quantities and make each fishcake half the size
Imam Bayeldi (page 93) – make half the quantity using baby aubergines
Mixed Vegetables with a Spicy Stuffing (page 100) – choose just one kind of vegetable
    rather than three
Mixed Pepper Tortilla (page 94) – halve the quantities
Three-Mushroom Risotto (page 95) – make half the quantity
Jumbo Pasta Shells with Tuna and Olives (page 109) – serve two shells per person

Starter Tips for Health

When choosing a starter for the sake of your figure and health, as well as for your enjoyment, remember *balance* is the key. In other words, choose something that will contrast well with your main course and provide complementary nutrients and a balance of calories.

For example, if your main course is high in protein, like the swordfish steaks on page 89, then the best starter is one high in carbohydrates, e.g. Watercress and Potato Soup (page 31). If your main course is relatively high in calories (and, perhaps, fat) choose a low-calorie, low-fat starter. For instance, Garlic Mushrooms (page 35) would be a sensible choice before Sizzling Beef Fajitas (page 49). And if your main course is low in calories and fat, then you may want to choose a more substantial starter, such as Tomatoes Stuffed with Pesto and Mozzarella (page 39) before Chilli Rice and Chickpeas (page 116). For more ideas on menu planning and balancing your diet, see the first chapter, Healthy Eating Made Simple.

Nutrition Notes

Most traditional restaurant and cookbook starters are high in both calories and fat. The following list shows the calorie and fat content of some of the most popular items and will help you to choose sensible starters and accompaniments.

CALORIE AND FAT COUNTS OF STARTERS AND ACCOMPANIMENTS

Eating out (All counts are average as portion sizes and recipes vary.)

	Cals	Fat (grams)
Avocado filled with prawns and mayonnaise	325	high
Avocado vinaigrette	275	high
Crab bisque	200	high
Deep-fried mushrooms	320	high
French onion soup	200	high
Garlic prawns in butter	250	high
Liver pâté and toast	400	high
Mozzarella and tomato	200	medium
Prawn cocktail	280	high
Smoked salmon (without bread)	80	medium
Smoked salmon pâté and toast	350	high
Taramasalata	200	high

At home

	Cals	Fat (grams)
Artichoke, globe (no butter)	20	trace
Asparagus, average serving	30	trace
Avocado, half a medium	125	12.5
Butter, melted, average serving	200	21.0
Crudités, average serving	20	trace
Goat's cheese, 25 g (1 oz)	47	3.6
Hummus, 50 g (2 oz)	90	6.0
Tzatziki, 50 ml (2 fl oz) serving	30	trace

Breads and spreads

	Cals	Fat (grams)
Bread or toast, 1 average slice	80	0.5
French bread, average 50 g (2 oz) portion	160	1.0
Garlic bread, average 50 g (2 oz) slice	200	5.0
Grissini (bread stick), one	15	trace
Pitta bread, 1 whole	185	2.2
Butter for 1 slice of bread	50	5.0
Low-fat spread for 1 slice of bread	20	2.0

French Provincial Soup with Tomato Pesto

SERVES 4

THIS classic recipe is completely delicious and very high in nutritional goodies, such as fibre and vitamins. However, don't ever serve it without the pesto, which is what makes it so wonderful. This is too filling for a starter, but makes a perfect lunch to share with friends. Don't be put off by the fairly long list of ingredients – the soup is simple to make.

1 tablespoon olive oil	100 g (3½ oz) precooked or drained canned flageolet or haricot beans
1 small onion, chopped	
1 medium leek, sliced	Salt and freshly ground black pepper
1.1 litres (2 pints) vegetable stock (see note)	**For the tomato pesto**
1 medium potato, weighing about 175 g (6 oz), peeled and chopped	2–3 good cloves garlic, peeled
	pinch of salt
2 celery stalks, chopped	good handful of fresh basil leaves
2 medium carrots, chopped	1 beef tomato or 3 regular tomatoes, skinned (see page 33), deseeded and chopped
200 g (7 oz) can chopped tomatoes	
25 g (1 oz) dried pasta shapes	60 g (2½ oz) Parmesan cheese, grated
100 g (3½ oz) French beans, cut into two	1 tablespoon olive oil
1 large (or 2 small) courgettes, sliced	

Heat the olive oil in a large, flameproof casserole. Add the onion and leek, and soften for 5 minutes, stirring from time to time. Add the stock, potato, celery, carrot and canned tomatoes, and simmer, covered, for 15 minutes.

Add the pasta, French beans and courgettes, and simmer for another 15 minutes. Lastly, stir in the beans, season with salt and pepper, and simmer for 2 minutes.

While the soup is cooking, make the pesto by pounding all the ingredients together with a pestle and mortar until you have a thick paste. Serve the soup in large bowls with the pesto in a small serving bowl. Let each person serve their own pesto so that they benefit from the gorgeous aroma as it melts into their soup!

NOTES AND TIPS

✦ *You can buy vegetable stock cubes but it is easy to make your own stock – simmer onions, carrots, celery and herbs in plenty of water for 45 minutes, strain and reduce.*

✦ *Serve the soup with crusty baguettes and finish with fresh fruit for a perfect lunch.*

NUTRITION

CALORIES PER PORTION: 265	PROTEIN: ★★★ FIBRE: ★★★ CARBOHYDRATE: ★★
TOTAL FAT PER PORTION: 11.5 g	VITAMINS: beta-carotene, C
SATURATED FAT PER PORTION: 4 g	MINERALS: K, Ca

Watercress and Potato Soup

SERVES 4

THIS easy and quick soup is packed full of flavour and very low in fat. The potatoes need to be an old, floury variety, such as King Edward or Wilja, so that they break up well during cooking.

The watercress should be very fresh and deep green; it is an excellent source of beta-carotene, vitamin C, iron and fibre.

600 ml (22 fl oz) chicken or vegetable stock	1 medium onion, finely chopped
450 g (1 lb) old potatoes, peeled and chopped	salt and freshly ground black pepper
2 good bunches of watercress, trimmed of tough stalks	1 heaped tablespoon low-fat crème fraîche
400 ml (¾ pint) skimmed milk	

Put the stock and potatoes in a saucepan and bring to the boil. Add the watercress, milk, onion, a little salt and plenty of black pepper. Cover and simmer for 20–30 minutes.

Remove from the heat and leave to cool for a few minutes, then purée in a blender for a few seconds. Return the soup to the pan, reheat and check the seasoning. Serve with a blob of crème fraîche in each bowl.

NOTES AND TIPS

✦ *Vary the soup by adding about 50 g (2 oz) peas with the watercress for more fibre and a sweeter taste.*

✦ *Try to add as little salt as you can to your cooking – like sugar, a taste for lots of salt is a habit that can easily be broken if you cut down gradually.*

NUTRITION

CALORIES PER PORTION: 145	PROTEIN: ★ FIBRE: ★★ CARBOHYDRATE: ★★★
TOTAL FAT PER PORTION: 1.5 g	VITAMINS: C, beta-carotene
SATURATED FAT PER PORTION: 0.5 g	MINERALS: K, Fe, Ca, Mg

Lentil and Bacon Soup

SERVES 4

HERE'S an ideal winter lunch that's perfect for weight-watchers as it is high in soluble fibre, the type of fibre that keeps hunger at bay for a *very* long time! This is real comfort food, especially when eaten with some dark rye bread.

1 tablespoon olive oil	1 medium carrot, chopped
100 g (3½ oz) lean unsmoked back bacon, derinded and chopped	1 clove garlic, peeled and chopped
	1 bay leaf
1 large onion, finely chopped	sprig of fresh thyme or 1 teaspoon dried thyme
300 g (11 oz) green or brown lentils, washed	salt and freshly ground black pepper
1 litre (1¾ pints) vegetable or chicken stock	fresh parsley sprigs, to garnish
1 large celery stalk, chopped	

Heat the oil in a non-stick frying pan, add the bacon and stir-fry until crisp. Remove the bacon from the pan with a slotted spoon and reserve for later. Add the onion to the frying pan and stir-fry until soft.

Transfer the onion to a saucepan and add all the remaining ingredients, except the bacon and parsley. Bring to the boil, then reduce the heat, cover and simmer for 1 hour or until the lentils are tender.

Allow the soup to cool a little, then remove the bay leaf and thyme sprig, if using, and pour half the soup into a blender. Blend until smooth, then return to the pan. Add the bacon pieces, stir well, and reheat before serving, garnished with parsley.

NOTES AND TIPS

◆ *You can omit the bacon if you like, reducing the calorie content to 305 per portion (5 g total fat; 0.5 g saturated).*

◆ *Or add croûtons instead of bacon. Brush 2 slices of wholemeal bread with 2 teaspoons olive oil, cut into squares and bake in the oven until crisp. Use as garnish. The calories per portion will then amount to 360; total fat slightly higher and saturated fat slightly lower than with the bacon.*

◆ *You can use chicken stock cubes, but they are quite salty. Make your own stock simply by simmering a chicken carcass with onion, carrot, celery and herbs in plenty of water for 1 hour. Strain and leave to get cold, then remove any fat which has risen to the surface. Boil to reduce for a stronger flavour.*

NUTRITION

CALORIES PER PORTION: 345	PROTEIN: ★★★ FIBRE: ★★★ CARBOHYDRATE: ★★★
TOTAL FAT PER PORTION: 7 g	VITAMINS: B group, C, beta-carotene
SATURATED FAT PER PORTION: 1.5 g	MINERALS: Fe, K, Mg

OPPOSITE   French Provincial Soup with Tomato Pesto (page 30), Onion Brushchetta (page 40)

Carrot and Tomato Soup

Serves 4

THIS soup is packed full of beta-carotene, vitamin C and all sorts of other good things. It's a real treat of a soup for everyone.

225 g (8 oz) good-quality, tasty, ripe tomatoes	450 ml (16 fl oz) vegetable stock
1 tablespoon groundnut oil	1 bay leaf
1 medium onion, finely chopped	salt and freshly ground black pepper
2 medium carrots, chopped	1 tablespoon dry sherry
1 clove garlic, peeled and chopped	handful of fresh basil leaves, chopped
½ teaspoon ground coriander	50 ml (2 fl oz) low-fat crème fraîche

Cut a cross in the top of each tomato and immerse in boiling water for 30 seconds. Drain, dip briefly into cold water, then slip off the skins. Chop the peeled tomatoes on a plate or board with a lip to catch the juice.

Heat the oil in a non-stick frying pan and add the onion. Stir over a medium heat until soft. Transfer the onion to a saucepan and add the carrots, tomatoes and their juice, garlic, coriander, stock, bay leaf, a little salt and plenty of black pepper. Cover, and simmer for 20 minutes.

Allow the soup to cool a little, then remove the bay leaf and purée the soup in a blender. Return to the pan, add the sherry and check the seasoning. Reheat gently. Swirl the basil into the soup with the crème fraîche before serving.

NOTES AND TIPS

✦ *For a spicier soup, add a dash of Tabasco.*
✦ *If you like fresh coriander, omit the basil and add chopped fresh coriander leaves.*
✦ *If you omit the crème fraîche and add low-fat Greek yogurt instead, you'll save 10 calories and 1 g fat per portion!*

NUTRITION

CALORIES PER PORTION: 90	PROTEIN: ★ FIBRE: ★★ CARBOHYDRATE: ★★
TOTAL FAT PER PORTION: 6 g	VITAMINS: beta-carotene, C
SATURATED FAT PER PORTION: 2 g	MINERALS: K

OPPOSITE   Sizzling Beef Fajitas with Salsa (page 49)

Bouillabaisse

SERVES 4

ALMOST more of a stew than a soup, this is one of those dishes that looks and tastes impressive but is quite easy to put together. It is also highly adaptable to whatever type of fish is available. The only requirement is that you need at least three different kinds of fish, plus some prawns. Choose firm white fish that doesn't disintegrate easily – cod, monkfish, swordfish, halibut, bream.

1 tablespoon olive oil	good pinch of saffron strands
1 large onion, finely chopped	1 bay leaf
1 large leek (or 2 small), sliced into thin rounds	½ teaspoon fennel seeds
1 large clove garlic, peeled and finely chopped	salt and freshly ground black pepper
2 large tomatoes (about 175 g/6 oz), skinned (see page 33)	900 g (2 lb) mixed filleted fish, cut into chunks (see above)
825 ml (1½ pints) good fish stock (see note)	175 g (6 oz) cooked peeled prawns
sprig of fresh thyme	handful of fresh parsley, chopped
piece of lemon or orange peel	

Heat the oil in a large sauté pan or flameproof casserole and stir-fry the onion and leek until soft. Add the garlic. Roughly chop the tomatoes and add to the pan with the stock, thyme, peel, saffron, bay leaf and fennel, and season with salt and pepper. Stir well, bring to a simmer and cook, uncovered, for 10 minutes.

Add the fish and simmer very gently for a further 10 minutes. Add the prawns and heat through. Remove the bay leaf and piece of peel. Serve topped with the parsley.

NOTES AND TIPS

✦ *You can easily make a fish stock by simmering the heads and bones of filleted fish in plenty of water with celery and carrot for 30 minutes (no longer). Strain well before using.*

✦ *If you don't have a large sauté pan or flameproof casserole, stir-fry the onion and leek in a non-stick frying pan, then transfer to a large saucepan before proceeding. You can, at a pinch, stir-fry the onions directly in the saucepan, but a good non-stick frying pan makes the job a lot easier when a reduced amount of oil is used.*

NUTRITION

CALORIES PER PORTION: 280
TOTAL FAT PER PORTION: 6 g
SATURATED FAT PER PORTION: 1 g

PROTEIN: ★★★ FIBRE: ★ CARBOHYDRATE: ★
VITAMINS: E, C, beta-carotene
MINERALS: K, Mg, Ca

Garlic mushrooms

SERVES 4

THIS easy starter, which can be served hot or cold, is low in calories but quite filling. I love garlic – but you've got to chop it *very* finely in this dish to get the right effect. Marinating the mushrooms for several hours improves their flavour – you could even make the dish a day ahead.

2 tablespoons olive oil	125 ml (4½ fl oz) passata (see note)
3 medium cloves garlic, very finely chopped	pinch of dark brown sugar
1 teaspoon ground coriander	salt and freshly ground black pepper
225 g (8 oz) small, perfect mushrooms (see note), trimmed, wiped and dried	1 pack of fresh coriander, de-stalked and chopped
2 tablespoons lemon juice	

Heat the oil in a small saucepan, add the garlic and ground coriander, and stir over a medium heat for a few minutes (but don't allow the garlic to brown). Add the mushrooms and stir to coat. Add the lemon juice, passata and sugar, and heat gently, stirring, to warm through. Season with black pepper and add half the fresh coriander.

Remove from the heat, put in a suitable container and leave to marinate for several hours (up to a day).

When you want to serve the mushrooms, check the seasoning and add a little salt if needed. Heat the mushrooms, if you like, or serve them cold. Sprinkle over the rest of the coriander, and serve with French bread.

NOTES AND TIPS
✦ *If you haven't any passata (sieved tomatoes, now available in cans, bottles or cartons in most supermarkets) you could mix 2 tablespoons tomato purée with 100 ml (3½ fl oz) water for a similar result.*
✦ *Parsley will do instead of coriander, but use the flat-leaved rather than the curly variety.*
✦ *Button mushrooms lack flavour – buy small (but not tiny) chestnut or brown cap mushrooms.*

NUTRITION

CALORIES PER PORTION: 85	PROTEIN: ★ FIBRE: ★★
TOTAL FAT PER PORTION: 8 g	CARBOHYDRATE (without bread): ★
SATURATED FAT PER PORTION: 1 g	VITAMINS: E, C
	MINERALS: K

Guacamole

SERVES 4

AVOCADOS have a bad name for being high in fat and calories. Yes they *are* high in fat (89 per cent of an avocado's calories are fat calories!) but it's mostly the good-for-you mono-unsaturated kind of fat. Avocados are also a good source of vitamin E, which isn't easy to get on a low fat diet. Serve this guacamole within an hour or so of making, otherwise it may lose its pretty green colour. Serve with pitta slices, grissini (bread sticks) and crudités.

1 large, ripe avocado	1 beef tomato, skinned (see page 33), deseeded and chopped
juice of 1 lime	
1 clove garlic, peeled and crushed, then chopped	2 spring onions, chopped
	dash of Tabasco sauce
1 good green chilli, deseeded and chopped	salt and freshly ground black pepper

Halve, stone, peel and chop the avocado and place in a bowl. Quickly add the lime juice and stir to coat (to prevent the avocado from going brown). Add the rest of the ingredients and mash well with a fork (an easy job if the avocado is ripe enough). Check the seasoning, and add more Tabasco if you prefer a 'hotter' guacamole.

NUTRITION

CALORIES PER PORTION: 120   PROTEIN: ★ FIBRE: ★★ CARBOHYDRATE: ★
TOTAL FAT PER PORTION: 11 g   VITAMINS: E, C, beta-carotene
SATURATED FAT PER PORTION: 1.5 g   MINERALS: Fe, K

Warm Artichoke Salad

SERVES 4

I INVENTED this one day when I had some canned artichoke hearts and green beans left over. It's a terrific starter, or an ideal side dish, without the dressing, to accompany fish.

1 tablespoon olive oil	**For the dressing**
1 large red pepper, deseeded and cut into thin strips	2 tablespoons olive oil
	2 teaspoons red wine vinegar
1 large leek, thinly sliced	pinch of caster sugar
400 g (14 oz) can artichoke hearts, drained, halved and dried on kitchen paper	pinch of mustard powder
	salt and freshly ground black pepper
150 g (5½ oz) cooked green beans, cut into 4 cm (1½ inch) lengths	
300 g (11 oz) can broad beans, drained or 190 g (6½ oz) cooked fresh or frozen beans	

To make the dressing, put all the ingredients in a screw-topped jar and shake well to combine. Alternatively, whisk the ingredients together in a jug or bowl.

For the salad, heat the oil in a non-stick frying pan and stir-fry the red pepper and leek over medium heat for a few minutes or until soft and the edges are just turning golden. Add the rest of the vegetables and stir gently for 2 minutes.

Turn the salad into serving bowls and drizzle a little dressing over each.

NOTES AND TIPS
✦ *You can add chunks of cooked salmon to the pan for a light lunch (adding 50 calories and 3.75 g fat for each 25 g/1 oz fish). With slices of brown bread, it's quite more-ish.*

NUTRITION

CALORIES PER PORTION: 170	PROTEIN: ★★ FIBRE: ★★ CARBOHYDRATE: ★★
TOTAL FAT PER PORTION: 11.5 g	VITAMINS: B group, C, beta-carotene, E
SATURATED FAT PER PORTION: 1.5 g	MINERALS: Ca, Fe, K

Smoked Trout Pâté

SERVES 4

NOTHING could be quicker than this pâté for a starter containing the special omega-3 fish oils (see page 76) and plenty of calcium.

175 g (6 oz) smoked trout fillet	pinch of caster sugar
2 teaspoons creamed horseradish	freshly ground black pepper
75 g (3 oz) 8 per cent fat fromage frais	salad leaves and tomato slices, to serve
2 level tablespoons 70 per cent fat-free mayonnaise-style dressing (see note)	4 sprigs watercress, to garnish
juice of ½ lemon	

Flake the trout into a bowl, removing any obvious fine bones. Add the remaining ingredients, except the salad, tomato and watercress. Mix well until thoroughly blended, then check the seasoning.

Arrange the salad leaves and tomato slices on serving plates, divide the pâté into four and pile on top. Garnish with watercress before serving.

NOTES AND TIPS
✦ *You can buy 70 per cent fat-free mayonnaise-style dressing under the Kraft brand name, or use any reduced-fat mayonnaise, which will add about 12 calories and 1.5 g fat per portion.*

NUTRITION

CALORIES PER PORTION: 88	PROTEIN: ★★★ FIBRE: ★ CARBOHYDRATE: ★
TOTAL FAT PER PORTION: 4.5 g	VITAMINS: B_3, C
SATURATED FAT PER PORTION: 2 g	MINERALS: Ca, K, Fe, Mg

Grilled Halloumi and Aubergine with Pitta

SERVES 4

I OWE this recipe to my love of Cyprus, where I became addicted to grilled halloumi. There, it is usually served with grilled bacon. This version is equally good, but much lower in saturated fat!

2 small aubergines, total weight about 400 g (14 oz)	freshly ground black pepper
2 tablespoons olive oil	8 stoned black olives, chopped
1 halloumi cheese, weighing about 200 g (7 oz)	2 wholemeal pitta breads, sliced
juice of 1 lemon	lemon wedges, to garnish

Slice the aubergines into 12 slices altogether. Blanch in boiling water for 1 minute, then drain and pat dry with kitchen paper. Brush a baking sheet with a little of the oil, and lay the aubergine slices on it. Brush the slices with the remaining oil, and grill under a medium heat for about 7 minutes or until golden. Turn and grill the other side until golden.

Meanwhile, slice the cheese into 8 or 12 slices and, when the aubergine is ready, arrange it in between the cheese slices in four small gratin dishes so that the cheese mostly covers the aubergine. Turn the grill to high. Put the gratin dishes under the grill for 1–2 minutes or until the cheese is golden.

Sprinkle the lemon juice, black pepper and olives over the cheese, and serve with pitta slices and lemon wedges.

NOTES AND TIPS

✦ *Halloumi is a medium-fat hard goat's cheese which often contains chopped mint leaves. It needs a very hot grill to brown it properly. If the grill isn't hot enough, the cheese stays white and just turns unpalatably hard. Cooked with care, it is a real delicacy.*

NUTRITION

CALORIES PER PORTION: 330	PROTEIN: ★★★ FIBRE: ★★ CARBOHYDRATE: ★
TOTAL FAT PER PORTION: 20 g	VITAMINS: C, E
SATURATED FAT PER PORTION: 7 g	MINERALS: Ca, K, Fe

Tomatoes Stuffed with Pesto and Mozzarella

SERVES 4

HOW I love this recipe with its gutsy explosion of rich pesto flavours, foiled perfectly by the cool, sweet tomato and bread! The mozzarella is just a lovely creamy bonus! This dish makes an excellent light lunch served with extra bread, and would make a good dinner-party starter served before a pasta main course.

2 beef tomatoes	a little salt
a little salt	1 pack fresh basil leaves
110 g (4 oz) half-fat mozzarella cheese	50 g (2 oz) Parmesan cheese, grated
1 heaped tablespoon breadcrumbs (see note)	2 tasty medium tomatoes, skinned (see page 33), deseeded and chopped
4 slices ciabatta, each weighing about 25 g (1 oz)	4 teaspoons olive oil
For the Pesto	1 tablespoon pine nuts
2 large cloves garlic, peeled	

First, preheat the oven to 200°C/400°F/Gas Mark 6 and make the pesto. Pound together all the ingredients, except the pine nuts, in a pestle and mortar. Stir in the pine nuts.

Halve the beef tomatoes (not through the stalk end) and scoop out the seeds (which could be added to a stew if you don't want to waste them). Sprinkle a little salt into each tomato half, and then divide the pesto evenly between them. Cut the cheese into four slices and top each tomato with a slice. Finally, sprinkle the breadcrumbs over the cheese.

Place the tomatoes on a baking sheet, and bake in the oven for 15 minutes or until the crumbs are golden and the cheese melted. The tomatoes should be soft but not mushy. Serve immediately with the *ciabatta*.

NOTES AND TIPS

✦ *Use stale bread to make the crumbs if you have any, because if the crumbs are too fresh they will still look pale and uninteresting when the cheese is melted.*

✦ *You could stuff large mushrooms in the same way, though the vitamin content of the dish would then be reduced.*

NUTRITION

CALORIES PER PORTION: 250	PROTEIN: ★★★ FIBRE: ★★ CARBOHYDRATE: ★
TOTAL FAT PER PORTION: 13.5 g	VITAMINS: beta-carotene, C, E
SATURATED FAT PER PORTION: 5 g	MINERALS: K, Ca, Mg

Onion Bruschetta

SERVES 4

I ADORE the flavours of the Mediterranean – onions, garlic, olives, olive oil – and here they all are, combined in a sublimely tasty and healthy starter or snack. The dish takes a while to make (you can't rush it), but it is *very* easy as long as you are patient.

2 tablespoons, plus 1 teaspoon olive oil	8 black olives, stoned and finely chopped
4 mild Spanish onions, thinly sliced into rings	1 tomato, deseeded (see page 33) and chopped
8 thickish slices olive ciabatta bread	few sprigs of flat-leaved parsley
1–2 cloves garlic, peeled, halved and lightly crushed	

Heat 2 tablespoons olive oil in a large non-stick frying pan over a medium heat. Add the onions and stir well for a few minutes or until softened.

Reduce the heat, cover the pan (with foil if you have no lid), and cook the onions as gently as possible for about 1 hour or until they are soft, moist and tender.

You can stir them from time to time but don't rush it – you don't want the onions to brown or crisp at all.

When the onions are ready, remove them from the heat and leave them, covered, in the pan while you grill the bread slices until golden. Brush the top of each slice of toast with the remaining 1 teaspoon olive oil, and rub the garlic well into each, leaving a few bits behind as you go. Put the slices on serving plates, then spoon the onion mixture evenly over them. Top each slice with some chopped olives, tomato and parsley, and serve straight away.

NOTES AND TIPS

✦ *The bruschetta can be eaten with your fingers; have plenty of napkins ready.*
✦ *Don't use strong English onions – they don't purée down so well or taste right in this dish.*
✦ *Try to buy the big, plump, juicy Greek black olives called kalamatas that you can buy loose from delis or in jars from most supermarkets.*

NUTRITION

CALORIES PER PORTION: 260	PROTEIN: ★ FIBRE: ★★ CARBOHYDRATE: ★★★
TOTAL FAT PER PORTION: 10 g	VITAMINS: C, E, beta-carotene
SATURATED FAT PER PORTION: 1.5 g	MINERALS: K, Ca

CHAPTER 4

MEAT

S ome people may hold their hands up in horror at finding a quite substantial chapter of meat recipes in a healthy-eating cookbook! Many of us wrongly assume that red meat cannot be part of a healthy diet, and that it contains high levels of saturated fat.

Certainly, what I call the 'old-fashioned' cuts of meat, such as pork belly, breast of lamb, and low-price minced beef, can be high in fat, saturated fat and calories. However, if you buy the right cuts and cook them in a healthy way, meat is not only *not* 'bad for you', but it can make an important contribution to the nutrients in your diet without adding much fat or calories.

Buy and cook lean!

Whenever you buy meat, choose the leanest cuts you can find. That way you can make the most of all the meat's goodness and avoid much of the saturated fat and calories. As an example, 25 g (1 oz) lean leg of lamb contains 40 calories and 2.2 g fat, while 25 g (1 oz) breast or shoulder contains 94 calories and 9 g fat. So go for all the lean cuts – beef, lamb and pork steaks instead of chops; extra-lean mince instead of standard mince; lean roasting joints instead of fatty ones; extra-lean bacon and low-fat sausages; and extra-lean braising steaks.

Lean meat is *less* fatty (and fattening) than many other protein sources, such as chicken with its skin, cheese, nuts or duck. A little lean meat goes a long way in my recipes, so you can afford to buy the best. Organic meat is ideal.

My recipes prove that there's no need to add tons of fat when cooking, especially when cooking meat. Here are some of the ways to cook lean: Think of meat as *part* of your meal, not the be-all and end-all of it. Whatever the recipe, add plenty of vegetables, pulses or grains, and so on. Meat is packed full of nutrients and flavour, so you don't need huge amounts.

✦ Use good quality utensils so there is no need to use masses of butter or oil for pre-browning, sautéing, etc. Use just enough.

✦ Add plenty of extra flavour in the form of spices and herbs, so that at the end of every meal you feel your tastebuds, as well as your appetite, have been well satisfied.

Quick Ideas for Healthy Meat Meals

✦ Marinate chunks of lean meat in natural low-fat yogurt mixed with spices, then grill.

✦ Sprinkle meat with ground spices or fresh herbs before grilling.

✦ Add a mustard and honey glaze to roasts.

✦ Make pockets in fillets of lamb or pork and stuff with dried fruits, leftover rice and seasoning.

To Make Beef Stock

Many of the recipes require a good beef stock. Many people use bought stock cubes, which can be a reasonable substitute, but most contain a lot of salt. It doesn't take long to make your own stock.

All you need is a bag of meat bones (*not* fatty trimmings), which you can get from your local butcher, some carrots, onion, celery and peppercorns. Put them in a large saucepan, cover with water and simmer gently for 2 hours. Strain, return the stock to the pan, and boil until reduced by half. Put in a container and cool. When the stock is cold, remove any visible fat from the surface.

Nutrition Notes

All meat (and offal) is a good source of 'complete' protein, but in other respects the different types of meat vary in their nutritional, fat and calorie content. The following is a quick rundown; see also the list on pages 43–44.

BEEF is especially rich in iron, zinc and vitamin B_{12}. Lean beef really is quite a low-fat food, containing only 4.2 g fatty acids per 100 g (3½ oz) meat. And it is higher in mono-unsaturated fats than it is in saturated fat!

Lean beef per 100 g (3½ oz): Total fat 4.2 g (saturated 45 per cent, mono-unsaturated 50 per cent, polyunsaturated 5 per cent); Cholesterol 59 mg; Potassium 350 mg; Iron 2.1 mg; Zinc 4.3 mg; good source of vitamins B_3, B_6 and B_{12}.

LAMB Lean lamb is the fattiest of the meats, containing nearly 8 g of fat per 100 g (3½ oz) lean meat.

Lean lamb per 100 g (3½ oz): Total fat 7.9 g (saturated 53 per cent, mono-unsaturated 41 per cent, polyunsaturated 6 per cent); Cholesterol 79 mg; Potassium 350 mg; Iron 1.6 mg; Zinc 4 mg; good source of vitamins B_2, B_3 and B_6.

PORK Lean pork is less fatty than lamb, despite its high-fat reputation. It is nearly as high in mono-unsaturates as beef, and is an even better source of B vitamins.

Lean pork per 100 g (3½ oz): Total fat 6.3 g (saturated 40 per cent, mono-unsaturated 44 per cent, polyunsaturated 16 per cent); Cholesterol 69 mg; Potassium 370 mg; Iron 0.9 mg; Zinc 2.4 mg; good source of vitamins B_1, B_2, B_3, B_6, B_{12}.

BACON Lean bacon is similar in fat content and nutrients to lean pork.

OFFAL The most popular offal, liver, is one of the best dietary sources of iron. However, because of its high cholesterol content it may not be suitable for people on a low-cholesterol diet, and because of its potentially toxic very high vitamin A content, it shouldn't be eaten by pregnant women.

Lamb's liver per 100 g (3½ oz): total fat 7.4 g (saturated 39 per cent, mono-unsaturated 40 per cent, polyunsaturated 21 per cent); Cholesterol 430 mg; Potassium 290 mg; Iron 9.4 mg; Zinc 3.9 mg; good source of vitamins B_1, B_2, B_3, B_6, B_{12} and folic acid; reasonable vitamin E content.

CALORIE AND FAT COUNTS FOR MEAT AND ACCOMPANIMENTS

Lean fresh meats, per 25 g (1 oz)

	Cals	Fat (grams)
Beef	30	1.1
Lamb	40	2.2
Pork	36	1.8
Bacon	37	1.8
Liver	45	2.5

Meat items

1 rump steak, lean only, 200 g (7 oz), grilled	335	12.0
1 chipolata sausage, grilled	75	5.0
Bacon, 1 back rasher, trimmed, grilled	75	4.7
Beefburger, 50 g (2 oz), grilled	115	9.0

Deli meats, per 25 g (1 oz)

Ham, lean	26	0.8
Mortadella	70	6.0
Parma ham	45	2.4
Pastrami	54	2.4
Pepperoni	61	4.3
Salami	110	10.0
Tongue	75	6.0

table continues

	Cals	Fat (grams)
Corned beef	59	3.1

Accompaniments

	Cals	Fat (grams)
Potato chips, average, 25 g (1 oz)	50	2.0
Roast potato, 1 average chunk	90	4.5
Baked potato, 225 g (8 oz)	170	trace
Plain boiled potato, 25 g (1 oz)	20	trace
Yorkshire pudding, average 50 g (2 oz) slice	100	5.0
Roast parsnip, 1 chunk	35	2.0
Mushrooms, fried, 25 g (1 oz)	40	4.0
Apple sauce, 2 teaspoons	10	trace
Horseradish, 2 teaspoons	23	1.2
Mint sauce, 2 teaspoons	10	trace
Gravy, 1 tablespoon, fat skimmed	15	1.0
Beef stock, 100 ml (3½ fl oz)	10	1.0

All green vegetables, plainly cooked, add only 3–7 calories per 25 g (1 oz) or 30 calories per average portion, maximum, and a trace of fat.

'Real' Chilli Con Carne with Rice

SERVES 4

I'VE called this recipe 'real' chilli con carne because far too much of what passes for chilli in homes and restaurants throughout the country is nothing like the real thing. Mostly, you get a mildly spiced tomato sauce with a few bits of minced beef and red beans floating in it. This one has proper pieces of meat in it and fresh chilli. And because there are plenty of beans and vegetables, it's a very well-balanced meal, nutritionally.

1 tablespoon corn oil	250 g (9 oz) ready-cooked dried or canned red kidney beans (see notes)
1 large onion, finely chopped	
1 large green pepper, deseeded and chopped into 1 cm (½ inch) squares	400 g (14 oz) can chopped tomatoes
	Tabasco sauce, to taste
325 g (12 oz) extra-lean braising steak, cut into very small cubes	salt and freshly ground black pepper
	225 g (8 oz) easy-cook mixed white and wild rice
300 ml (11 fl oz) beef stock	
2 tablespoons tomato purée	good handful fresh coriander, chopped
2 green chillies, deseeded and finely chopped (see note)	

Heat the oil in a large non-stick frying pan and stir-fry the onion and pepper until soft. Add the beef and cook, stirring, for a few minutes or until brown.

Add the rest of the ingredients, except the rice and half the coriander, stir, and bring to a simmer. Cover, and cook gently for 1½ hours or until the meat is tender and you have a rich sauce. Check once or twice during cooking that there is enough liquid – if not, add a little water or more beef stock.

When the meat is tender, check the seasoning; if you prefer a hotter chilli, add more Tabasco.

Cook the rice as instructed on the packet. Serve the chilli with the rice, scattered with the remaining coriander.

NOTES AND TIPS

+ *If you prefer, you can stir-fry the onions and pepper in a shallow flameproof casserole, and then cook the chilli in the oven at 170°C/325°F/Gas Mark 3.*
+ *One 400 g (14 oz) can red kidney beans will yield about 250 g (9 oz) drained weight of beans; 75 g (3 oz) dried beans will yield about 250 g (9 oz) when cooked. Before cooking dried beans, soak them in water for 8 hours, then fast-boil in fresh water for 10 minutes before simmering until tender (about 1½ hours).*

NUTRITION

CALORIES PER PORTION: 420	PROTEIN: ★★★ FIBRE: ★★ CARBOHYDRATE: ★
TOTAL FAT PER PORTION: 9 g	VITAMINS: B$_3$, C
SATURATED FAT PER PORTION: 2.5 g	MINERALS: K, Zn, Ca

Hungarian Beef Goulash

SERVES 4

IF I HAD to pick one best-ever family beef recipe, this would probably be it. It proves that just because a dish contains red meat and cream, and tastes wonderful, it doesn't have to be high in fat. This version is particularly low-fat and virtuous.

3 teaspoons corn oil	300 ml (11 fl oz) beef stock
450 g (1 lb) extra-lean braising steak, cubed	400 g (14 oz) can plum tomatoes
2 medium onions, roughly chopped	100 ml (3½ fl oz) red wine
2 tablespoons Hungarian paprika	salt and freshly ground black pepper
1 tablespoon plain flour	550 g (1¼ lb) floury potatoes, peeled and cut
1 teaspoon caraway seeds	into 2.5 cm (1 inch) cubes
1 large red pepper, deseeded and sliced	40 ml (1½ fl oz) half-fat crème fraîche
1 red chilli, deseeded and chopped (optional)	fresh coriander leaves, to garnish

Heat 2 teaspoons oil in a flameproof casserole or lidded sauté pan and brown the meat a bit at a time. (Don't stir the pieces of meat around until they have sealed or they may stick.) Remove to a plate.

Add the rest of the oil to the pan and stir-fry the onions until soft. Add the paprika and flour, and stir for 1 minute. Add the caraway seeds, red pepper, chilli, stock, tomatoes with their juice, and the wine, and season with salt and pepper. Return the beef to the pan and stir well. Bring to a simmer, cover and cook for 1½ hours (or in the oven at 170°C/325°F/Gas Mark 3).

Add the cubed potatoes to the pan and simmer for 30 minutes more or until tender. Serve with the crème fraîche drizzled over, and garnished with coriander leaves.

NOTES AND TIPS

✦ *If you are very hungry you may want to serve some rice or crusty bread with the goulash.*

NUTRITION

CALORIES PER PORTION: 400	PROTEIN: ★★★ FIBRE: ★★ CARBOHYDRATE: ★★
TOTAL FAT PER PORTION: 11 g	VITAMINS: B group, beta-carotene, C, E
SATURATED FAT PER PORTION: 4.5 g	MINERALS: Fe, K

Italian Beef in Red Wine

SERVES 4

HERE'S another meal that seems indulgent (because of the wine), but isn't. It also contains plenty of fibre and vitamins.

1 tablespoon corn oil	250 g (9 oz) ready-cooked or canned haricot or borlotti beans
450 g (1 lb) extra-lean braising steak in 4 pieces	2 medium carrots, sliced
20 shallots, peeled	225 g (8 oz) mixed mushrooms
2 cloves garlic, peeled and crushed	4 medium tomatoes, skinned (see page 33) and quartered
salt and freshly ground black pepper	275 ml (½ pint) Italian red wine
1 tablespoon plain flour	bouquet garni
150 ml (5½ fl oz) beef stock	

Heat the oil in a flameproof casserole and brown the steaks over a high heat. Remove to a plate. Stir-fry the shallots to brown, then add the garlic, season with salt and pepper, add the flour, and stir for 1 minute.

Add the beef stock and stir again to mix well. Add the beans, carrots, mushrooms and tomatoes, then the wine and bouquet garni. Stir gently, cover and simmer for 1½ hours or until the steak is tender. Remove the bouquet garni before serving.

NOTES AND TIPS

✦ *Serve with new potatoes and a green vegetable.*

--- NUTRITION ---

CALORIES PER PORTION: 340   PROTEIN: ★★★ FIBRE: ★★ CARBOHYDRATE: ★
TOTAL FAT PER PORTION: 10 g   VITAMINS: B group, beta-carotene, C, E
SATURATED FAT PER PORTION: 3.5 g   MINERALS: Fe, K

Beef and Mixed Pepper Stir-Fry

SERVES 4

HERE'S how to make a little steak go a long way. Stir-frying retains much of the vitamin C in the vegetables and ensures you use little oil, but if you're on a low-salt diet, beware of adding too much soy sauce to stir-fries.

225 g (8 oz) medium egg thread noodles	dash of Tabasco sauce
1 tablespoon sesame or groundnut oil	1 tablespoon soy sauce
325 g (12 oz) beef steak, e.g. rump, cut into strips	1 small knob of fresh root ginger, peeled (see note)
450 g (1 lb) mixed peppers, deseeded and sliced	1 teaspoon runny honey
200 ml (7 fl oz) beef stock	pinch of Chinese five-spice powder
100 g (3½ oz) baby sweetcorn	1 teaspoon cornflour

Put the noodles on to soak in boiling water (or follow packet instructions). Meanwhile heat the oil in a wok and stir-fry the beef and peppers over a high heat until browned. Add a little stock and the corn. Stir-fry for 1 minute, then add the Tabasco, soy sauce, ginger, honey and five-spice powder. Stir-fry for 2 minutes, adding a little beef stock from time to time.

Finally, mix the cornflour with the remaining beef stock and add to the pan. Stir until bubbling. Drain the noodles and add to the pan. Stir for a minute and serve.

NOTES AND TIPS

+ *If you like a mild gingery taste, keep the ginger in one whole piece and remove before serving. If you like a stronger ginger taste, chop the piece of ginger finely before adding to the stir-fry. Ginger aids digestion and helps speed up your metabolic rate.*
+ *Sesame oil gives stir-fries a lovely nutty taste and distinctive aroma.*

NUTRITION

CALORIES PER PORTION: 420	PROTEIN: ★★★ FIBRE: ★★ CARBOHYDRATE: ★★★
TOTAL FAT PER PORTION: 10 g	VITAMINS: B group, beta-carotene, C, E
SATURATED FAT PER PORTION: 3.5 g	MINERALS: Fe, K

Sizzling Beef Fajitas with Salsa

SERVES 4

MEXICAN food is normally brimful of fat, but this dish isn't because I've used extra-lean beef and minimum 'sizzling' oil, and I haven't brushed the tortillas with oil as is often recommended – it's not necessary. So you have all the taste but half the fat. This is *exactly* what healthy cooking should be about.

325 g (12 oz) lean rump steak, cut into thin strips

1–2 fresh red chillies, deseeded and chopped

2 cloves garlic, peeled and chopped

juice of 1 lime

handful of fresh coriander, chopped

8 ready-made wheat tortillas (325 g/12 oz pack)

1 tablespoon corn oil

1 medium Spanish onion, halved and thinly sliced

1 red pepper, deseeded and sliced

1 green pepper, deseeded and sliced

1 teaspoon taco seasoning

100 ml (3½ fl oz) half-fat crème fraîche

For the salsa

1 beef tomato, skinned (see page 33), deseeded and finely chopped

4 cm (1½ inch) piece of cucumber, finely chopped

1 small red onion, finely chopped

handful of fresh coriander, chopped

pinch of ground coriander

juice of 1 lime

freshly ground black pepper

First, make the salsa. Mix all the ingredients together, spoon into a serving bowl, cover and leave in the fridge.

Put the beef strips in a shallow bowl with the chillies, garlic, lime juice and coriander. Mix well, cover and leave to marinate for 1 hour.

When you are ready to cook the beef, put the tortillas, well wrapped in foil, into the oven at 170°C/375°F/Gas Mark 3 to warm through (or seal them in microwave film and heat them in the microwave according to packet instructions).

Remove the beef from the bowl, reserving the marinade left in the bowl. Heat the oil in a non-stick frying pan and brown the beef over a high heat for 1 minute. Remove with a slotted spoon and keep warm. Stir-fry the onion and peppers, again over a high heat, until starting to char. Return the beef to the pan with any juices and with any reserved marinade. Add the taco seasoning, and sizzle for another 1–2 minutes. Serve with the tortillas, the salsa and the crème fraîche drizzled over each beef portion.

--- **NUTRITION** ---

CALORIES PER PORTION: 495
TOTAL FAT PER PORTION: 17 g
SATURATED FAT PER PORTION: 7.5 g

PROTEIN: ★★★ FIBRE: ★★ CARBOHYDRATE: ★★
VITAMINS: beta-carotene, C, E, B group
MINERALS: Fe, K

Beef Stroganoff and Noodles

SERVES 4

FOR a quick, yet luxurious, supper-party dish, this is ideal. Stroganoff is usually very high in fat, but by using minimum oil instead of maximum butter, and by substituting low-fat Greek yogurt for high-fat sour cream, I've made it a much better balanced meal – but still creamy and delicious.

15 g (½ oz) low-salt butter	2 teaspoons plain flour
2 teaspoons corn oil	1 tablespoon brandy
1 medium onion, finely chopped	250 ml (9 fl oz) beef stock
250 g (9 oz) dried tagliatelle or fettuccine	pinch of caster sugar
325 g (12 oz) extra-lean rump steak, cut into strips	salt and freshly ground black pepper
	150 ml (5½ fl oz) low-fat Greek yogurt
325 g (12 oz) small mushrooms	paprika, to garnish
2 teaspoons sweet paprika	

Melt the butter in a large non-stick frying pan with the oil. Add the onion, and sauté over a medium heat until it is soft and just turning golden. Meanwhile, cook the noodles in a saucepan of lightly salted boiling water for about 8 minutes or until tender.

When the onions are soft, remove them from the pan with a slotted spatula and keep warm. Turn the heat up, add the meat to the pan and brown on all sides. Turn the heat down, and return the onion to the pan with the mushrooms, paprika and flour. Stir for 1 minute, then add the brandy, stock and sugar. Simmer, uncovered, for 5 minutes, then add salt and pepper to taste.

Before serving, drain the noodles and arrange on a heated serving dish. Add the yogurt to the frying pan and stir through. Serve the beef on the noodles with paprika sprinkled over.

NOTES AND TIPS
+ *You can also use fillet of pork in this dish.*
+ *Try Dijon mustard instead of the paprika for a change.*
+ *For a completely balanced meal, serve with a mixed or green side salad.*

NUTRITION

CALORIES PER PORTION: 460   PROTEIN: ★★★ FIBRE: ★★ CARBOHYDRATE: ★★★
TOTAL FAT PER PORTION: 13 g   VITAMINS: B group, C
SATURATED FAT PER PORTION: 4.5 g   MINERALS: Fe, Ca
Note: This dish contains 136 mg cholesterol per portion.

Turkish Lamb Kebab Pittas

SERVES 4

EVER since I first tasted a version of this in the Middle East years ago, it has been a firm favourite. You wouldn't believe that anything so simple and with so few ingredients could be so more-ish. I've cut fat from the original version by toasting the pine nuts (instead of frying them), and by using the leanest lamb and low-fat Greek yogurt. Even if you think you're not a yogurt fan, you'll love this!

15 g (½ oz) pine nuts	1 large clove garlic, peeled and crushed, then chopped
1 tablespoon olive oil	
450 g (1 lb) lean lamb fillet (leg or neck), cut into bite-sized strips	250 ml (9 fl oz) low-fat Greek yogurt
	4 wholemeal pitta breads
1 teaspoon ground cumin	few leaves fresh flat-leafed parsley
salt and freshly ground black pepper	
1 large beef tomato, skinned (see page 33) and chopped	

Spread the pine nuts on a baking sheet and toast under the grill for a few minutes or until lightly golden – watch them carefully or they will burn!

Heat the oil in a non-stick frying pan and brown the lamb pieces over a high heat. Turn the heat down a little, add the cumin and a little salt, stir and cook for a few more minutes or until the lamb is just cooked. Remove the lamb from the pan and keep warm.

Add the tomato and garlic to the pan and stir for a few minutes. Season with salt and pepper, then spoon into a shallow serving bowl. Arrange the lamb pieces on top and keep warm. Heat the yogurt gently in a clean saucepan and pour over the lamb. Top with the pine nuts, grind over some black pepper, garnish with parsley, and serve with the pittas, warmed and halved. Scoop the lamb mixture up with the pittas!

NOTES AND TIPS

✦ *You could also split open the pitta breads and fill them with the mixture.*

✦ *The lamb mixture can also be used to top rice or baked potatoes. A 200 g (7 oz) baked potato or 200 g (7 oz) boiled rice will give the meal a similar nutritional value (omitting the pittas).*

NUTRITION

CALORIES PER PORTION: 490	PROTEIN: ★★★ FIBRE: ★★ CARBOHYDRATE: ★★
TOTAL FAT PER PORTION: 20 g	VITAMINS: B₃, C, beta-carotene, C, E
SATURATED FAT PER PORTION: 7.5 g	MINERALS: K, Zn, Fe, Ca

Lamb Cannellini

SERVES 4

THIS quick casserole is full of Mediterranean flavour. Served with a big plateful of rice, or a baked potato, it makes a nice supper for a cool evening. Try to use as many pulses as you can in your casseroles – they add tons of fibre and mean you can get away with using less meat.

1 tablespoon olive oil	400 g (14 oz) can chopped tomatoes
450 g (1 lb) lean lamb fillet (leg or neck), cut into chunks	pinch of dark brown sugar
	1 bay leaf
4 shallots, peeled (see page 54) and chopped	few sprigs of fresh parsley
1 large clove garlic, crushed	few sprigs of fresh thyme
2 teaspoons plain flour	salt and freshly ground black pepper
1 tablespoon lemon juice	400 ml (¾ pint) lamb stock (see note)
75 ml (3 fl oz) dry white wine	
400 g (14 oz) can cannellini beans, drained and rinsed, or 250 g (9 oz) cooked dried cannellini beans (see note)	

Heat the oil in a flameproof casserole or lidded sauté pan. Add the lamb and brown over a high heat for 1 minute, then add the shallots, turn down the heat, and cook, stirring, until the shallots have softened.

Add the garlic, stir for 1 minute, then stir in the flour. Add the lemon juice and wine, and stir until bubbling. Add the beans, tomatoes, sugar and herbs, and season with salt and pepper. Add some of the stock, stir and bring to a simmer. Cover and cook for 1 hour, adding a little more lamb stock as necessary. You want to end up with a rich sauce, not too much liquid.

NOTES AND TIPS

✦ *You could try using other beans, e.g. borlotti or butter beans. Remember, if cooking your own beans, they need pre-soaking for several hours and fast boiling for the first 10 minutes. Don't add salt to the boiling water – it will toughen the beans.*

✦ *If you can't get lamb stock, or have none that you've made yourself from lamb bones and vegetables, use weak beef stock. If you do make your own stock, always remember to allow it time to get cold so that you can remove any fat that rises to the top as it cools.*

NUTRITION

CALORIES PER PORTION: 335	PROTEIN: ★★★ FIBRE: ★★ CARBOHYDRATE: ★
TOTAL FAT PER PORTION: 14 g	VITAMINS: B_3, B_6, beta-carotene, C, E
SATURATED FAT PER PORTION: 6 g	MINERALS: Zn, Fe, K, Ca, Mg

Moroccan Lamb Casserole

SERVES 4

THIS is a hefty humdinger of a main meal for hungry people – full of fibre and iron, yet not at all high in calories, and very low in fat. I love its sweet and savoury taste – plus the fact that it is easy to cook.

1 tablespoon olive oil	825 ml (1½ pints) lamb stock
450 g (1 lb) lean lamb fillet (leg or neck), cubed	1 sachet saffron strands
	110 g (4 oz) ready-to-eat dried apricots
1 large onion, sliced, or 12 shallots, peeled	50 g (2 oz) ready-to-eat dried apple rings
1 clove garlic, peeled and crushed	400 g (14 oz) can chickpeas, drained and rinsed, or 250 g (9 oz) cooked dried chick-
1 teaspoon ground cinnamon	peas (see note)
1 teaspoon ground cumin	1 tablespoon lemon juice
2 teaspoons plain flour	
salt and freshly ground black pepper	

Heat the oil in a large flameproof casserole, add the lamb pieces and brown over a high heat. Remove the lamb from the pan and keep warm.

Add the onion to the pan, and stir-fry over a medium heat for a few minutes or until softened. Add the garlic, cinnamon and cumin, and stir for 1 minute. Add the flour and stir again, then season with salt and pepper. Return the lamb to the pan, and add the stock and saffron. Stir, add the apricots and apples, chickpeas and lemon juice, stir again, cover and simmer for 1 hour. Check the seasoning and serve.

NOTES AND TIPS

+ *The best thing to serve with this casserole is steamed couscous, with some chopped coriander and a few sultanas added. A chicory salad would also go well.*
+ *This dish can also be made using pork fillet.*
+ *If cooking dried chickpeas, remember they need very long soaking (12 hours) before you boil them. And don't add salt to the boiling water or they will be very tough.*

NUTRITION

CALORIES PER PORTION: 405

TOTAL FAT PER PORTION: 14 g

SATURATED FAT PER PORTION: 6 g

PROTEIN: ★★★ FIBRE: ★★★ CARBOHYDRATE: ★★

VITAMINS: B group

MINERALS: Zn, Fe, K, Ca, Mg

Note: This dish contains 90 mg cholesterol per portion.

Spicy Red Kebabs with Tomato Sauce

SERVES 4

THIS heartwarming plateful bursts with flavour. I love it when I hit upon a really gorgeous sauce that tastes wicked, but isn't – and this is it.

1 red onion	½ teaspoon dried oregano
450 g (1 lb) lean lamb fillet (leg or neck), cubed	1 bay leaf
	salt and freshly ground black pepper
2 tablespoons lemon juice	125 ml (4½ fl oz) passata
1 tablespoon olive oil	1 medium aubergine
2 cloves garlic, peeled and crushed, then chopped	1 medium red pepper, deseeded and cut into squares
½ teaspoon ground cumin	40 g (1½ oz) low-fat Greek yogurt
½ teaspoon brown sugar	
½ teaspoon dried thyme	

Cut the onion in half round its middle (not through the root end) and then into quarters. Separate the 'leaves' of onion and put them in a bowl with the lamb. Combine the rest of the ingredients, except the aubergine, red pepper and yogurt, and pour over the lamb and onion, stirring to mix. Leave to marinate for 2–4 hours.

Two hours before cooking time, peel and cube the aubergine, place in a colander and sprinkle with salt. Place a weighted plate on top and leave to drain for about 30 minutes.

Rinse the aubergine and pat dry with kitchen paper. Wash your hands and scoop the lamb and onion out of the marinade, then thread the meat and vegetables prettily on to kebab skewers. Pour the marinade into a small saucepan. Grill the kebabs under a medium high heat for about 10 minutes, turning once. Meanwhile, cook the marinade ingredients for 1–2 minutes stirring, until heated through. Before serving, remove the bay leaf and stir in the yogurt. Serve the kebabs with the sauce poured over.

NOTES AND TIPS

◆ *These kebabs go extremely well with pilau rice (or plain boiled basmati) and a cool green salad to offset all that red! You could also eat them with pittas or crusty Greek-style bread.*

NUTRITION

CALORIES PER PORTION: 270	PROTEIN: ★★★ FIBRE: ★★ CARBOHYDRATE: ★
TOTAL FAT PER PORTION: 14 g	VITAMINS: B$_3$, folic acid, C, beta-carotene, E
SATURATED FAT PER PORTION: 6 g	MINERALS: Zn, Fe, K, Ca

Moussaka

SERVES 4

ANOTHER of my favourite meat dishes. Normally high in fat and low on flavour and inspiration, moussaka can be a disaster gastronomically and nutritionally. This low–fat version, however, is delicious, and protein- *and* mineral-packed. Remember that healthy eating isn't *just* about cutting fat – it's also about getting enough important nutrients.

2 medium–large aubergines	25 g (1 oz) low-fat spread
salt and freshly ground black pepper	25 g (1 oz) plain flour
2 tablespoons olive oil	1 teaspoon mustard powder
2 medium onions, finely chopped	400 ml (14 fl oz) skimmed milk
1 large clove garlic, peeled and chopped	75 g (3 oz) half-fat Cheddar-style cheese, grated
400 g (14 oz) lean lamb, minced	
1 teaspoon dried mixed Mediterranean herbs	1 size-3 egg, beaten
1 tablespoon tomato purée	2 heaped tablespoons breadcrumbs
about 150 ml (5½ fl oz) lamb or beef stock	1 tablespoon freshly grated Parmesan cheese

Slice the aubergines into rounds and place in a colander, sprinkling each layer with salt. Cover with a weighted plate and leave to drain for 30 minutes. Rinse the aubergine slices and pat dry with kitchen paper. Use half the oil to brush the slices and either dry-fry in a non-stick frying pan, bake or grill until browned.

Heat the remaining oil in a non-stick frying pan, add the onions and sauté until soft and transparent but just turning golden. Add the garlic and minced lamb, and stir-fry until the lamb is brown. Add the herbs, tomato purée and stock, season with salt and pepper, and simmer for 45 minutes, stirring occasionally and adding a little extra stock or water if the mixture looks too dry. Check the seasoning, then pile the mixture into an ovenproof dish and top with the aubergine slices.

Preheat the oven to 190°C/375°F/Gas Mark 5. Meanwhile, make the topping, melt the low-fat spread in a non-stick saucepan, add the flour, and cook, stirring, for 2 minutes over a medium heat. Add the mustard, and gradually add the milk, stirring all the time, until you have a smooth sauce. Season with salt and pepper, add the grated cheese, and stir to melt. Add the beaten egg and mix well, then pour the sauce over the aubergines, smoothing to coat evenly. Sprinkle with breadcrumbs and Parmesan, and bake in the oven for 40 minutes or until the top is golden and bubbling.

NOTES AND TIPS

✦ *You could use boiled potato slices instead of the aubergine, saving 4 g fat but adding an extra 42 calories per portion.*

--- NUTRITION ---

CALORIES PER PORTION: 425	PROTEIN: ★★★ FIBRE: ★★ CARBOHYDRATE: ★
TOTAL FAT PER PORTION: 24 g	VITAMINS: B$_3$, folic acid, C, A, D, E
SATURATED FAT PER PORTION: 9 g	MINERALS: Zn, Fe, Ca, K

Note: This dish contains 150 mg cholesterol per portion.

Venison and Mushroom Casserole

SERVES 4

I'M pleased that venison is becoming more widely available because, to my mind, it is even tastier than beef – *and* it is higher in iron and lower in saturates and total fat. It is also tender and easy to cook. This big-flavoured casserole is my favourite way to cook it. The wine and brandy are a bit of a luxury, but for a special-occasion dinner, who's worried?

1 tablespoon corn oil	1 tablespoon plain flour
450 g (1 lb) cubed venison	50 ml (2 fl oz) brandy
12 shallots, peeled	100 ml (3½ fl oz) red wine
1 large green pepper, deseeded and chopped	1 heaped tablespoon tomato purée
2 cloves garlic, peeled and crushed	salt and freshly ground black pepper
1 bay leaf	150 ml (5½ fl oz) beef stock
a few sprigs of fresh thyme	225 g (8 oz) chestnut mushrooms
4 juniper berries	

Heat the oil in a flameproof casserole, add the venison, and cook on high heat until browned. Remove the venison from the pan with a slotted spatula and keep to one side. Add the shallots to the casserole and fry until brown. Add the green pepper and garlic, and stir for another few minutes, then return the venison to the pan and add the herbs and juniper berries. Add the flour and stir well, then add the brandy and wine, stirring again until the casserole is bubbling.

Add the tomato purée, and season with salt and pepper. Pour in the stock, and bring to a simmer. Cover, and simmer very slowly for 1½ hours (or cook the casserole in the oven at 150°C/300°F/Gas Mark 2). Add the mushrooms to the casserole, stir and continue cooking for a further 30 minutes. Check the seasoning and serve.

NOTES AND TIPS

+ *This is a rich-tasting casserole that goes well with simple accompaniments such as mashed potato and white cabbage, or any plain green vegetable.*
+ *You could use lean braising steak instead of venison in this recipe, too.*
+ *Because venison is a low-fat meat it needs to be cooked very slowly and gently in a casserole – the wine and brandy in this recipe help keep the meat very tender and succulent (the acid acts as a marinade).*

NUTRITION

CALORIES PER PORTION: 300	PROTEIN: ★★★ FIBRE: ★★ CARBOHYDRATE: ★
TOTAL FAT PER PORTION: 10 g	VITAMINS: B group, C, beta-carotene, E
SATURATED FAT PER PORTION: 3.5 g	MINERALS: Fe, K, Ca

Pork Tenderloins in Spicy Mustard Sauce

SERVES 4

PEOPLE always think of pork as fattening, but the lean cuts certainly aren't, and pork contains only 40 per cent saturated fat (of its total fat content). Tenderloins (or fillets) are great for quick cooking; serve this easy supper with plenty of rice and green salad for a low-fat, low-calorie treat.

1 tablespoon groundnut oil	2 teaspoons Dijon mustard
325 g (12 oz) tenderloin of pork, sliced into rounds	pinch of caster sugar
	2 teaspoons lemon juice
1 medium onion, finely chopped	salt and freshly ground black pepper
1 medium red pepper, deseeded and cut into diamond shapes	150 g (5½ oz) button mushroom, or larger mushrooms, sliced
1 teaspoon garam masala	4 tablespoons low-fat Greek yogurt
25 ml (1 fl oz) dry white wine	2 tablespoons chopped fresh parsley
1 teaspoon cornflour	
200 ml (7 fl oz) chicken stock	

Heat the oil in a non-stick frying pan, add the pork, and cook quickly over a high heat until browned. Remove the pork from the pan with a slotted spatula. Add the onion and red pepper to the pan, and stir for a few minutes. Lower the heat, return the pork to the pan, add the garam masala and wine, and stir well. Simmer for a few minutes.

Stir the cornflour into the stock and add to the pan with the mustard, sugar and lemon juice. Season with salt and pepper, and simmer for a few more minutes. Add the mushrooms and cook for 2 minutes, then stir in the yogurt and half the parsley. Serve with the remaining parsley sprinkled over the top.

NOTES AND TIPS

✦ *You can make this dish using skinned chicken or turkey instead of the pork, too.*
✦ *Hungry non-slimmers could use the recipe to serve 2–3 people.*

NUTRITION

CALORIES PER PORTION: 235	PROTEIN: ★★★ FIBRE: ★ CARBOHYDRATE: ★
TOTAL FAT PER PORTION: 11 g	VITAMINS: B group, C, beta-carotene, E
SATURATED FAT PER PORTION: 3.5 g	MINERALS: Fe, Mg, K

Pork and Cider Pie

SERVES 4

—

SWEET yet acidic and savoury, this dish is a simple, low-fat winner.

2 teaspoons corn oil

4 pork fillet steaks, each weighing about 175 g (6 oz), cut into 2–3 pieces each

12 shallots, peeled, or 1 large mild onion, finely chopped

100 ml (3½ fl oz) chicken stock, plus extra to cover

2 medium carrots, chopped into quite small chunks

2 medium eating apples, cored and sliced into rounds

275 ml (½ pint) dry cider

25 g (1 oz) plain flour

salt and freshly ground black pepper

good handful of fresh parsley, roughly chopped

650 g (1½ lb) potatoes, peeled, parboiled and sliced into thick rounds

Preheat the oven to 170°C/325°F/Gas Mark 3. Meanwhile, heat the oil in a non-stick frying pan, swirling the pan around to spread the oil in a thin coating all over the bottom of the pan and up the sides. Add the pork, and brown the underside without moving the meat until it is well sealed (or it will stick). Turn and brown the other side.

Add the shallots or onion to the pan with a very little of the chicken stock, and stir well, simmering for 1 minute.

Transfer the meat and onion to a flameproof casserole and add the carrots, apples and cider. Sift the flour over and season with salt and pepper. Add the parsley, and cover the whole lot with a layer of potatoes. Pour on the rest of the chicken stock, and if the stock doesn't just barely cover the potatoes, add more until it does.

Put the lid on and bake in the oven at 170°C/325°F/Gas Mark 3 for 1 hour, making sure you have a tight seal. Remove the lid and brown the top of the potatoes under the grill.

NOTES AND TIPS
✦ *Serve with a green vegetable such as broccoli or spring greens.*
✦ *Wild boar would make an interesting substitute for the pork in this recipe.*
✦ *If you're slimming, you can reduce the calories in this healthy dish even more by using half the cider and increasing the chicken stock, and by using 150 g (5½ oz) pork steaks and adding a little more carrot instead. You'll save around 100 calories per portion.*

NUTRITION

CALORIES PER PORTION: 500   PROTEIN: ★★★ FIBRE: ★★ CARBOHYDRATE: ★★
TOTAL FAT PER PORTION: 15 g   VITAMINS: B group, C, beta-carotene, E
SATURATED FAT PER PORTION: 5 g   MINERALS: Zn, Fe, K, Ca
Note: This dish contains 120 mg cholesterol per portion.

Bacon and Vegetable Gratin

SERVES 4

HERE'S the perfect family supper. Bacon is a wonderful source of B vitamins, and if you choose the extra-lean, reduced-salt kind it can easily be part of a healthy diet. Always cook it until it is crisp, though, so that as much fat as possible runs out. It's nicer that way, anyhow.

275 g (10 oz) extra-lean, low-salt back bacon, derinded	700 ml (1¼ pints) skimmed milk
1 cauliflower, cut into medium florets	110 g (4 oz) half-fat Cheddar-style cheese
1 head of broccoli, cut into medium florets	1 teaspoon mustard powder
450 g (1 lb) potatoes	salt and freshly ground black pepper
4 medium tomatoes	2 tablespoons dry breadcrumbs
40 g (1½ oz) low-fat spread	1 tablespoon freshly grated Parmesan cheese
40 g (1½ oz) plain flour	

Cut each bacon slice into two and grill or dry-fry until crisp and golden. Parboil the cauliflower and broccoli separately in lightly salted water until barely tender – don't overcook. Drain. Peel and cut the potatoes into 2.5 cm (1 inch) chunks and boil in lightly salted water until just tender. Drain. Chop two of the tomatoes and slice the remaining two into rounds.

Preheat the oven to 190°C/375°F/Gas Mark 5. Melt the low-fat spread in a small saucepan and stir in the flour. Cook, stirring, for 1–2 minutes, then gradually add the milk, stirring as you do so, until you have a smooth sauce. Add the cheese and mustard, season with salt and pepper, and stir well.

To assemble the gratin, arrange the vegetables in a suitable baking or gratin dish, with the bacon pieces tucked in between and the chopped tomatoes scattered over. Pour the sauce evenly over the top and scatter the breadcrumbs and grated Parmesan cheese over the sauce. Arrange the sliced tomatoes around the edge. Bake in the oven for 20 minutes or until the top is golden.

NOTES AND TIPS

✦ *You could use cooked pasta instead of the potatoes for a dish of similar nutritional value.*

NUTRITION

CALORIES PER PORTION: 450	PROTEIN: ★★★ FIBRE: ★★ CARBOHYDRATE: ★★
TOTAL FAT PER PORTION: 16 g	VITAMINS: B group, C, beta-carotene, E, D
SATURATED FAT PER PORTION: 7 g	MINERALS: Ca, K, Fe

CHAPTER 5

CHICKEN AND TURKEY

Chicken still outsells every other type of meat in this country, and turkey is rapidly gaining in popularity too, as we become more used to the idea that it's not just something to roast on festive occasions. Lower-cost, mass-market chickens are fine used in casseroles and curries as they tend to 'soak up' other flavours well. For plain cooking – grilling or roasting – and for salads, however, I would recommend buying a free-range or corn-fed chicken. Their flavour is superior and worth the extra expense.

Quick Ideas for Healthy Poultry Meals

✦ Sprinkle barbecue seasoning on chicken joints with some lemon juice, then bake and serve with rice.

✦ Coat turkey steaks with Cajun seasoning and fry in a very little corn oil.

✦ Spread whole grain mustard on skinned chicken pieces and grill.

✦ Cook chicken or turkey fillets in foil or parchment parcels with herbs, citrus juice, seasonings and thinly sliced leeks and carrots.

✦ If dry-frying poultry, add a dash of wine to the pan juices and bubble before serving.

Chicken Stock

Chicken stock made from cubes is acceptable as a standby, but it is usually very salty. It is easy to make your own.

Instead of buying ready-prepared chicken portions, buy a whole chicken, joint it yourself (it's very easy) and use the carcass to make stock. Put it in a large saucepan with celery, carrots, leeks, onion, some rosemary, thyme and peppercorns, cover with water, and simmer for 1 hour, removing any scum. Strain and cool. When cold, remove any fat that has risen to the top. The stock can be reduced if you like before storing and to concentrate the flavours. It will keep in the fridge for 1–2 days, or it will freeze. A good tip is to freeze concentrated stock in ice cube containers so that you can thaw just as much or as little as you need.

Nutrition notes

Poultry has a reputation for being a very good, low-fat source of protein. Indeed, it *is* a good protein source, but it is only a low-fat food if you remember to remove the skin before eating and, preferably, before cooking. With it's skin on, chicken contains 230 calories per 100 g (3½ oz) and 16.7 g fat, compared with 123 calories and 4.2 g fat for lean beef. But with no skin, chicken goes down to 121 calories per 100 g (3½ oz) and only 4 g fat. Turkey meat is even lower in fat and calories than lean chicken – 107 calories per 100 g (3½ oz) and a mere 2 g of fatty acids per 100 g (3½ oz).

Both chicken and turkey meat are a little lower in saturated fats than red meat – 35 per cent for both. Lean chicken has 57 mg cholesterol per 100 g (3½ oz), and is a good source of potassium, magnesium and vitamins B_3 and B_6. Turkey has 61 mg cholesterol per 100 g (3½ oz), and is a good source of potassium, magnesium, zinc and vitamins B_3, B_6 and B_{12}.

CALORIE AND FAT COUNTS FOR POULTRY AND ACCOMPANIMENTS

Fresh poultry, per 25 g (1 oz) unless otherwise stated

	Cals	Fat (grams)
Chicken, meat only	30	1.0
Chicken, lean and skin	57	4.2
Turkey, meat only	27	0.5
Breast of chicken portion, average, skin on	228	17.0
Breast of chicken portion, average, skin removed	120	4.0

Accompaniments

1 tablespoon meat stuffing	30	2.0
1 tablespoon non-meat stuffing	15	1.0
2 teaspoons cranberry sauce	20	trace
1 cocktail sausage	40	3.0
1 slice streaky bacon	100	7.0
1 tablespoon traditional bread sauce	25	1.5

Provençal Baked Chicken and Vegetables

SERVES 4

THIS recipe almost cooks itself, and is a pleasant change from ordinary roast chicken and boiled veg. Roasting vegetables retains more of their vitamin C than boiling or steaming, and concentrates the flavour.

4 chicken breast portions, skinned	sprigs of fresh rosemary, thyme and oregano, or 1 teaspoon dried of each
juice of 1 lemon	
2 tablespoons olive oil	salt and freshly ground black pepper
2 cloves garlic, peeled and chopped	1 large aubergine
1 red pepper, deseeded and cut into quarters	4 medium courgettes
1 yellow pepper, deseeded and cut into quarters	1 red onion, cut into 8 wedges

Make two or three slashes in each chicken breast, and place in a shallow dish. Sprinkle on the lemon juice and ½ tablespoon olive oil and rub well in. Fill the slashes with the garlic, peppers and herbs, and finally, sprinkle a little salt over. Cover and leave to marinate for 1 hour.

Meanwhile, slice the aubergine into rounds and cut each round into half. Cut the courgettes into 2.5 cm (1 inch) chunks. Place the aubergine and courgettes in a colander, and sprinkle with salt. Put a weighted plate on top and leave to drain for 30 minutes or more. This draws out any bitter juices. Rinse and pat dry with kitchen paper.

Preheat the oven to 190°C/375°F/Gas Mark 5. Toss all the vegetables, including the onion, in the remaining oil to coat well, then arrange in a baking tray in one layer. Grind on some black pepper, and bake in the oven for 20 minutes.

Take the tray out of the oven, turn the vegetables and add the chicken breasts to the tray, spooning over them any marinade remaining in the dish. Bake for a further 20–25 minutes or until the chicken and vegetables are tender and golden, basting the chicken with the pan juices at least once. Serve at once.

NOTES AND TIPS

✦ *Instead of salting and draining the chopped aubergine and courgette you can blanch them for 30 seconds in boiling salted water and then pat dry. Aubergines and courgettes aren't always bitter, but if they are to be roasted, it's wise to salt or blanch them first.*

✦ *In winter you can roast different vegetables. I love sweet potato and pumpkin chunks with parsnip and red onions – a selection very high in beta-carotene.*

NUTRITION

CALORIES PER PORTION: 280
TOTAL FAT PER PORTION: 13 g
SATURATED FAT PER PORTION: 3 g

PROTEIN: ★★★ FIBRE: ★★ CARBOHYDRATE: ★
VITAMINS: B_3, B_6, beta-carotene, C, E, folic acid
MINERALS: K, Ca

Mexican Chilli Chicken

SERVES 4

Low in calories but high in mono-unsaturated and polyunsaturated fats, this is a delicious taste of Mexico. Avocados are full of vitamin E, and well worth incorporating in your healthy diet.

1½ tablespoons corn oil	½ teaspoon ground coriander
4 skinless chicken breast portions, each cut into two, or 8 boned, skinned chicken thighs	400 g (14 oz) can chopped tomatoes
	2 tablespoons wine vinegar
1 large green pepper, deseeded and chopped into 1 cm (½ inch) pieces	1 teaspoon dark brown sugar
1 Spanish onion, finely chopped	1 teaspoon Tabasco sauce
1 large clove garlic, peeled and finely chopped	salt and freshly ground black pepper
2 fresh green chillies, deseeded and finely chopped	1 medium avocado
	juice of 1 lime
2 tablespoons chopped fresh coriander	25 ml (1 fl oz) tomato juice

Heat ½ tablespoon of the oil in a non-stick frying pan, add the chicken pieces and cook until browned. Transfer the chicken to a shallow ovenproof dish (such as a lasagne dish). Put the green pepper in the frying pan, stir-fry for 1 minute, then scatter over the chicken.

Heat the remaining oil in the same pan, and sauté the onion, garlic and chillies until the onion is soft and just turning golden. Add the fresh and ground coriander, the tomatoes, wine vinegar, sugar and Tabasco, and season with salt and pepper. Stir well and simmer gently, uncovered, for 30 minutes or until you have a thick sauce.

Meanwhile, halve, stone and peel the avocado and cut it into 12 chunks, then toss immediately in the lime juice in a small bowl.

Preheat the oven to 190°C/375°F/Gas Mark 5. Pour any excess lime juice into the cooked tomato sauce, and if the sauce is too thick to pour, thin with the tomato juice. Pour the sauce over and around the chicken pieces, and bake, uncovered, in the oven for 25 minutes. Remove from the oven and gently push the avocado chunks down amongst the chicken pieces so that you can still see them, then return the dish to the oven and cook for a further 10 minutes. Serve immediately.

NOTES AND TIPS

✦ *Serve with warm tortillas, or rice, and a green salad. You could also have a salsa if you like (try the one on page 49).*

NUTRITION

CALORIES PER PORTION: 310	PROTEIN: ★★★ FIBRE: ★★ CARBOHYDRATE: ★
TOTAL FAT PER PORTION: 16 g	VITAMINS: B_3, B_6, beta-carotene, C, E
SATURATED FAT PER PORTION: 4 g	MINERALS: K, Mg

French Country Chicken Casserole

SERVES 4

YOU'LL love this recipe, which is ideal for family eating but also special enough to serve at a dinner party. I'm totally in love with Dijon mustard in my savoury cooking; it can transform a dish and adds depth, smoothness, richness, flavour and heat all in one small package! I've used whole grain Dijon here because it gives the dish added texture and visual appeal. When you cook the dish, do a taste test: try the casserole sauce just before you add the mustard, and again afterwards, then you'll see what I'm talking about.

1 tablespoon corn oil	450 ml (16 fl oz) chicken stock
4 boned skinless chicken joints (leg or breast), each cut into 2	100 ml (3½ fl oz) skimmed milk
	salt and freshly ground black pepper
12 shallots, peeled	4 canned artichoke hearts, drained and halved
6 small carrots, cut lengthways into quarters	1 tablespoon whole grain Dijon mustard
2 medium leeks, cut into rounds	
1 tablespoon plain flour	

Preheat the oven to 170°C/325°F/Gas Mark 3. Heat half the oil in a non-stick frying pan, add the chicken pieces and cook over a high heat, without moving them, for 1 minute or until golden. Turn and repeat. Transfer the chicken to an ovenproof casserole.

Stir-fry the shallots in the frying pan for 1–2 minutes or until tinged golden. Add to the casserole with the carrots and leeks. Heat the remaining oil in a non-stick saucepan (adding any remaining oil from the frying pan, too), and stir in the flour with a wooden spoon. Cook over a medium heat for 1 minute, stirring, then gradually add the stock, stirring as you go. When the stock is in, add the milk, with salt and pepper, season and stir. Pour over the chicken and cook in the oven for 30 minutes. Add the artichokes to the casserole and cook for a further 20 minutes or until everything is tender. Transfer the chicken and vegetables to a serving plate. Stir the mustard into the sauce and serve.

NOTES AND TIPS

✦ *You can use ordinary smooth mustard or tarragon mustard, if you like, but* don't *use English; it will be far too hot!*

✦ *Make sure the casserole only simmers; don't let it reach a fast bubble.*

✦ *Instead of the artichoke hearts you could substitute tender celery hearts, but add them at the start of cooking. You can also try pheasant breasts instead of the chicken.*

✦ *I serve this with potatoes and green beans.*

NUTRITION

CALORIES PER PORTION: 295	PROTEIN: ★★★ FIBRE: ★★ CARBOHYDRATE: ★
TOTAL FAT PER PORTION: 9 g	VITAMINS: B group, C, E, beta-carotene
SATURATED FAT PER PORTION: 2.5 g	MINERALS: K, Ca

Chicken Paprika

SERVES 4

THIS is a real hybrid of a recipe – something like an Italian cacciatore, a bit like a marengo, and a lot like traditional paprika chicken. Whatever – it is good. Paprika is another of those spices that is totally indispensable in the health-conscious kitchen; it adds so much warmth, richness and flavour for virtually no calories or fat.

2 tablespoons olive oil	400 g (14 oz) can plum tomatoes
4 boneless chicken breast or leg joints, skinned	1 tablespoon tomato purée
1 large Spanish onion, roughly chopped	125 ml (4½ fl oz) dry white wine
2 cloves garlic, peeled and crushed	1 teaspoon dried mixed Mediterranean herbs
1 tablespoon plain flour	175 g (6 oz) courgettes, sliced
2 teaspoons Hungarian paprika	salt and freshly ground black pepper
2 tablespoons brandy	225 g (8 oz) button mushrooms
200 ml (7 fl oz) chicken stock	

Heat a third of the oil in a flameproof casserole, add the chicken joints and cook until brown. Remove the chicken from the pan.

Add the rest of the oil to the casserole and sauté the onion and garlic until the onion is soft and just turning golden. Add the flour and paprika, and stir for 1 minute, then add the brandy and stir again. Pour in the stock, and add the tomatoes with their juice, the tomato purée, wine, herbs and courgettes. Season with salt and pepper, stir well, cover and simmer for 40 minutes (or you could cook in the oven at 170°C/325°F/Gas Mark 3.

Add the mushrooms to the casserole and stir, then simmer for a further 15 minutes before serving.

NOTES AND TIPS

✦ *This dish is so low in fat that you could afford to stir in a little half-fat crème fraîche before serving. Two tablespoons (for the whole dish) would add just over 1 g of fat and 13 calories per portion.*

NUTRITION

CALORIES PER PORTION: 325	PROTEIN: ★★★ FIBRE: ★★ CARBOHYDRATE: ★
TOTAL FAT PER PORTION: 13 g	VITAMINS: B_3, B_6, C, beta-carotene, E
SATURATED FAT PER PORTION: 3 g	MINERALS: K, Ca

OPPOSITE PAGE 64 Provençal Baked Chicken and Vegetables (page 62)
OPPOSITE Normandy Chicken (page 66)

Normandy Chicken

SERVES 4

TRADITIONAL Normandy chicken (or pork) is very high in saturated fat because it uses lashings of butter and double cream, and the skin is left on the meat. As this recipe proves, all that fat just isn't necessary.

15 g (½ oz) butter	275 ml (½ pint) dry cider
1 tablespoon corn oil	a few sprigs of fresh thyme or 1 teaspoon dried thyme
4 chicken breast fillets, skinned	
2 eating apples	salt and freshly ground black pepper
pinch of sugar	2 tablespoons half-fat crème fraîche
8 shallots, peeled and sliced	sprigs fresh parsley, to garnish
1 tablespoon brandy or Calvados (see note)	

Heat the butter and oil in a sauté pan with a lid (or a flameproof casserole), add the chicken breasts and cook until browned. Meanwhile, core the apples and slice them into rounds.

Remove the chicken from the pan with a slotted spatula. Add the apple slices to the pan with the sugar, and fry for 1 minute on each side. Remove from the pan. Add the shallots to the pan and stir-fry for 2 minutes to soften slightly. Return the chicken to the pan with the brandy, and stir for 1 minute. Add the cider, thyme and apple rings, and season with salt and pepper. Bring to a simmer, cover and simmer gently for 25 minutes.

Remove the chicken, onions and apple rings from the pan with a slotted spatula, turn up the heat, and boil the pan liquid to reduce. Meanwhile, arrange the onions and apple rings on serving plates. Cut each chicken breast into five slices, arrange on the plates with the onions and apple, and keep warm. When the pan liquid is reduced to a thinnish sauce, add the cream, stir, check the seasoning and pour over or around the chicken. Garnish with parsley and serve immediately.

NOTES AND TIPS

✦ *Tenderloin of pork will give around the same nutritional values as chicken.*
✦ *Serve with boiled potatoes and green vegetables.*

NUTRITION

CALORIES PER PORTION: 310	PROTEIN: ★★★ FIBRE: ★ CARBOHYDRATE: ★
TOTAL FAT PER PORTION: 13 g	VITAMINS: B$_3$, B$_6$
SATURATED FAT PER PORTION: 5 g	MINERALS: K

Spanish Chicken

SERVES 4

THIS is similar to a paella but there's much less emphasis on the rice. The traditional versions from the Mediterranean have masses more oil and high-fat sausage, but you can cut down on these quite happily and still enjoy a robust dish – one of my top three chicken dishes ever, I think! You'll need a very large flameproof pan, preferably with a lid. Otherwise, cook it in two pans.

2 tablespoons olive oil	8 slices (about 25 g/1 oz) mini pepperoni (see note)
4 chicken leg or breast joints, skinned and each cut into 2	1 teaspoon dried mixed Mediterranean herbs
450 g (1 lb) small onions (*not* shallots), each weighing about 100 g (3½ oz), quartered	300 ml (11 fl oz) chicken stock
	25 ml (1 fl oz) orange juice
2 red peppers, deseeded and diced	1 sachet saffron strands, steeped in a little water
225 g (8 oz) long-grain rice	
2 tomatoes, chopped	150 ml (5½ fl oz) dry white wine
25 g (1 oz) sun-dried tomatoes, drained of oil and chopped	8 black olives, stoned and chopped
2 cloves garlic, peeled and chopped	

Heat the oil in a large, lidded sauté pan, add the chicken pieces, and cook until lightly browned. Remove to a plate. Add the onion quarters to the pan, and cook, stirring, until they are tinged with gold, then add the red peppers and stir-fry for 1–2 minutes. Add the rice and stir well.

Add all the remaining ingredients (including the saffron water), except the olives. Return the chicken to the pan, just put it on top of everything else, and finally scatter the olives over the top. Bring to a gentle simmer, making sure that the rice is thoroughly covered with liquid. Put the lid on and simmer for 1 hour, checking occasionally that the rice isn't getting too dry. If it is, add some more chicken stock or water. Serve when the rice and chicken are both very tender.

NOTES AND TIPS

If you can't get pre-packed mini pepperoni slices, use 25 g (1 oz) any Italian or Spanish sausage and slice it into eight. The pre-packed mini slices are very handy, though, for making sure that you don't over-estimate.

NUTRITION

CALORIES PER PORTION: 570	PROTEIN: ★★★ FIBRE: ★★ CARBOHYDRATE: ★★★
TOTAL FAT PER PORTION: 15.5 g	VITAMINS: B_3, B_6, beta-carotene, C, E
SATURATED FAT PER PORTION: 3.5 g	MINERALS: K, Zn

Coq au Vin

SERVES 4

TRADITIONALLY, coq au vin is made with a whole bottle of wine, fatty bacon, fatty croûtons and masses of butter and oil; and the skin is left on the chicken. I think this lighter version is actually *better* than the original! Serve with plain potatoes, French beans and broccoli.

1 free-range or corn-fed chicken, weighing about 1.3 kg (3 lb), cut into 8 joints, skin removed, wings discarded	4 tablespoons brandy
	½ bottle (375 ml/12 fl oz) red wine
1 heaped tablespoon plain flour	250 ml (9 fl oz) chicken stock
salt and freshly ground black pepper	2 cloves garlic, peeled and crushed
2 tablespoons corn oil	1 bouquet garni
350 g (12½ oz) shallots, peeled	75 g (3 oz) bread
110 g (4 oz) lean unsmoked gammon rasher, chopped	225 g (8 oz) mushrooms
	roughly chopped fresh parsley, to garnish

Put the chicken pieces in a large plastic bag with the flour. Season with salt and pepper, and shake to coat.

Heat the oil in a large non-stick frying pan, add the shallots, and stir-fry until lightly browned. Transfer the shallots to a flameproof casserole. Add the gammon to the frying pan, and stir-fry for 1 minute, then transfer to the casserole. Add the chicken pieces to the frying pan and brown lightly.

Pour the brandy over the chicken and set it alight. (Don't panic!) When the flames die down, transfer the chicken and any juices to the casserole, plus any flour left in the bag. Add the wine, stock, garlic and bouquet garni to the casserole, stir, cover and simmer for 1¼ hours.

While the chicken is cooking, crumble the bread roughly and scatter on a baking tray. Bake in the oven at 180°C/350°F/Gas Mark 4 for 10–15 minutes or until crisp and golden. Set aside, uncovered, until ready to serve.

When the chicken has been simmering for 1¼ hours, add the mushrooms, and simmer for a further 15 minutes. When cooked, remove and discard the bouquet garni. Check the seasoning, arrange the chicken, onions, mushrooms and bacon on serving plates or a single platter, and keep warm. If necessary, boil the pan liquid until you have a rich sauce. Check the seasoning. Pour the sauce over or around the chicken, and scatter the bread and parsley on top.

NUTRITION

CALORIES PER PORTION: 470	PROTEIN: ★★★　FIBRE: ★★　CARBOHYDRATE: ★
TOTAL FAT PER PORTION: 15 g	VITAMINS: B group, C, E
SATURATED FAT PER PORTION: 4 g	MINERALS: K

Chicken Chow Mein

SERVES 4

AT THE Chinese take-away, chow mein will undoubtedly include fried noodles, but in China the noodles are usually left 'soft', as here – a nice contrast to the crisp vegetables.

250 g (9 oz) chicken breast fillet, skinned and sliced into 4 cm (1½ inch) strips	50 g (2 oz) mangetout or baby sweetcorn
1 tablespoon soy sauce	100 g (3½ oz) fresh beansprouts
2 tablespoons dry sherry	100 g (3½ oz) small mushrooms, sliced
1 clove garlic, peeled and crushed	8 small spring onions, trimmed
1 small knob of fresh root ginger, peeled and finely chopped	75 g (3 oz) Chinese leaves, thinly sliced
	200 ml (7 fl oz) chicken stock
275 g (10 oz) medium egg noodles (dry weight)	50 g (2 oz) cooked peeled prawns
1 tablespoon sesame or groundnut oil (see note)	2 teaspoons cornflour mixed with a little chicken stock
1 large red pepper, deseeded and sliced into 2.5 cm (1 inch) strips	

Put the chicken strips in a shallow bowl with the soy sauce, sherry, garlic and ginger. Cover, and leave to marinate for 1 hour.

Meanwhile, gather together all the remaining ingredients and prepare the vegetables, ready for cooking. Cook or soak the noodles in a large pan of boiling water, depending on the packet instructions. When ready, drain nearly all of the water away and keep the noodles warm in a colander set over a pan of water over a low heat.

Heat the oil in a wok, add the chicken (reserving the marinade), and stir-fry over a high heat for 1 minute or until browned. Add the red pepper, and cook, stirring constantly, for 2 minutes. Add the mangetout or sweetcorn and stir-fry for another minute, then add the remaining vegetables and a little stock, and stir-fry for 1 minute. Add the chicken marinade and prawns and stir-fry again for another minute, finally adding the rest of the chicken stock and the cornflour. Allow to bubble, turn the heat down and simmer for 30 seconds while you arrange the noodles on serving plates or a single platter. Top with the chicken mixture, then toss lightly to amalgamate some of the noodles with the chicken and vegetables. Serve at once.

NOTES AND TIPS

✦ *Sesame oil is delicious with a fabulous aroma. It is worth investing in a 500 ml (1 pint) bottle just for stir-fries. It is high in mono-unsaturates, as is groundnut (peanut) oil.*

NUTRITION

CALORIES PER PORTION: 445	PROTEIN: ★★★ FIBRE: ★★ CARBOHYDRATE: ★★★
TOTAL FAT PER PORTION: 12 g	VITAMINS: B₃, B₆, C, beta-carotene
SATURATED FAT PER PORTION: 3 g	MINERALS: K

Turkey and Cashew Chilli Stir-Fry

SERVES 4

CASHEWS, like all nuts, are high in fat, but it is mostly mono-unsaturated, and nuts are a rich source of vitamin E, which isn't that easy to find in the average diet. They are also rich in iron and other minerals, so don't give up on nuts just because they are calorific.

375 g (12 oz) turkey stir-fry strips	250 g (9 oz) broccoli, cut into small florets
1 clove garlic, peeled and chopped	1 fresh red chilli, deseeded and finely chopped
1 teaspoon runny honey	25 ml (1 fl oz) orange juice
1 tablespoon soy sauce	2 teaspoons cornflour
1 tablespoon sesame oil	125 ml (4½ fl oz) chicken stock
1 red onion, sliced	50 g (2 oz) raw unsalted cashew nuts
1 large carrot, cut into thin strips	

Put the turkey strips in a shallow container with the garlic, honey and soy sauce, cover, and leave to marinate for 30 minutes or more.

Heat the oil in a wok and add the turkey (reserving any marinade), onion and carrot. Stir-fry for 2 minutes, then turn down the heat and add the broccoli, chilli and orange juice. Stir-fry for 2 minutes.

Stir the cornflour into the chicken stock, and add to the wok with any reserved turkey marinade. Add the nuts and stir-fry for 1–2 minutes. Serve immediately.

NOTES AND TIPS

◆ *Serve with plenty of rice.*

NUTRITION

CALORIES PER PORTION: 260   PROTEIN: ★★★ FIBRE: ★★ CARBOHYDRATE: ★
TOTAL FAT PER PORTION: 12 g   VITAMINS: B$_3$, B$_6$, beta-carotene, C, E
SATURATED FAT PER PORTION: 2.5 g   MINERALS: K, Fe, Mg, Ca

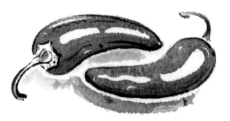

Aromatic Turkey with Citrus Sauce

SERVES 4

THIS is a real no-fuss dish for a quick supper, containing almost no saturated fat.

1½ tablespoons corn or sunflower oil	1 small knob of fresh root ginger, peeled and very finely chopped
2 teaspoons lemon juice	a few sprigs of fresh thyme
1 clove garlic, peeled and crushed, then chopped	juice and grated rind of 1 orange
salt and freshly ground black pepper	1 teaspoon runny honey
4 turkey steaks, each weighing about 140 g (5 oz) and cut into 4 diagonal slices	1 teaspoon cornflour mixed with a little water

Mix 1 tablespoon of the oil with the lemon juice and garlic. Add some black pepper, and use to coat the turkey. Leave to marinate for 30 minutes or more.

Heat the remaining oil in a non-stick frying pan, add the turkey steaks (reserving the marinade), and cook until brown on all sides. Turn down the heat and add the reserved marinade, the ginger, thyme, orange juice and rind, and honey. Season with salt, stir, cover and simmer for 10 minutes.

Remove the steaks to warm serving plates and add the cornflour mixture to the pan. Simmer, stirring, until thickened. Pour the sauce over or around the steaks and serve.

NOTES AND TIPS

✦ *When grating rind from citrus fruits, be sure not to include any of the white pith as it is very bitter.*

✦ *This recipe also works well with lean pork steaks.*

✦ *Serve with new potatoes and green beans or mangetout.*

NUTRITION

CALORIES PER PORTION: 215	PROTEIN: ★★★ FIBRE: ★ CARBOHYDRATE: ★
TOTAL FAT PER PORTION: 8 g	VITAMINS: B_3, B_6, C
SATURATED FAT PER PORTION: 1.5 g	MINERALS: K

Garlic Chicken Roast

SERVES 4

HERE'S a treat for the taste-buds – and your heart. Even if you think you don't like too much 'good for you' garlic, give this a try as, when roasted properly, garlic is mild, nutty and delicious. For once, the skin is left on the chicken, but there's little other fat in the dish.

1 small/medium roasting chicken, preferably free-range	2 teaspoons garlic purée
	1 tablespoon olive oil
1 lemon	40 plump, fresh cloves of garlic, unpeeled
a few sprigs of fresh thyme or 2 teaspoons dried thyme	150 ml (5½ fl oz) chicken stock
	2 teaspoons plain flour
3 cloves garlic, peeled and crushed	
salt and freshly ground black pepper	

Preheat the oven to 190°C/375°F/Gas Mark 5.

Remove the giblets (you can make stock with these, see note) and any fat clinging to the inside of the bird. Snip the wings off with kitchen scissors; you don't want to roast these. Place the chicken in the middle of a piece of foil large enough to enclose the bird completely. Halve the lemon and squeeze the juice into a jug, then pop the squeezed lemon halves inside the chicken cavity with half the thyme, the crushed cloves of garlic and some black pepper. Rub the garlic purée all over the outside of the bird, then pour the lemon juice and olive oil over evenly. Sprinkle with a little salt, plenty more black pepper, and the rest of the thyme.

Arrange the whole, unpeeled garlic cloves all around the base of the chicken, fold up the foil, and seal to form a loose but airtight parcel. Place in a roasting tin, and bake in the oven for 1 hour.

Take the tin from the oven, open the foil (enjoy the aroma), and baste the chicken well with the pan juices. Crumple the foil up around the bird so that the bird remains uncovered, return to the oven and roast for about another 20 minutes or until the chicken is golden and the juices run clear when a thigh is pierced with a skewer. Test an unpeeled garlic clove: pick it up in your fingers and suck the clove – the inside should be melty. Eat that and discard the skin.

Remove the chicken and garlic cloves to a serving platter and keep warm while you make some gravy. Pour the juices from inside the foil into the roasting tin, skim off any visible fat from the top and add the chicken stock mixed with the flour. Stir over a high heat until the gravy is bubbling, then serve with the chicken.

NOTES AND TIPS

✦ *To make stock, simmer the giblets in water with onion, carrot and celery for 1 hour. Strain and season.*

✦ *The total fat count given for this dish is for a portion including half an average serving of the chicken skin, and half of the fat left in the pan gravy. If you eat no chicken skin and manage to skim all the fat off the pan gravy, the fat and calorie content will be lower. If, however, you eat all of your portion of skin and skim no fat from the gravy, it will be higher.*

✦ *Any leftover chicken, stock or gravy will make a delicious, garlicky soup. If you add gravy to the soup, let it go cold first so you can skim any fat off the top.*

NUTRITION

CALORIES PER PORTION: 400
TOTAL FAT PER PORTION (SEE ABOVE): 25 g
SATURATED FAT PER PORTION: 8.5 g

PROTEIN: ★★★ FIBRE: ★ CARBOHYDRATE: ★
VITAMINS: B_3, B_6
MINERALS: K

Note: This dish contains 80 mg cholesterol per average portion.

Chicken in Barbecue Sauce

SERVES 4

SWEET and sour is one of my favourite flavour combinations, and a good sweet-sour sauce is one of the cleverest ways to disguise the fact that you're not adding much fat.

2 teaspoons olive oil	dash of Tabasco sauce
1 small onion, finely chopped	1 teaspoon mustard powder
1½ tablespoons Worcestershire sauce	½ teaspoon garlic purée (optional)
2 tablespoons brown sugar	100 ml (3½ fl oz) water or chicken stock
1½ tablespoons wine vinegar	salt and freshly ground black pepper
2 heaped tablespoons tomato ketchup	8 skinned chicken thighs, boned or bone-in

Preheat the oven to 190°C/375°F/Gas Mark 5.

Put all the ingredients, except the salt and pepper and chicken thighs, in a blender, and blend to a smooth sauce. Heat in a small saucepan and bubble for 1 minute. Taste and add a little seasoning, if needed.

Put the chicken in a shallow baking dish (not too large). Pour the sauce all over and around the chicken, making sure it gets right underneath and coats well over the top. Cover the dish and bake in the oven for 20 minutes, then remove the cover, baste thoroughly and bake for a further 15 minutes. Serve immediately.

NOTES AND TIPS

✦ *This is ideal served with lots of plain boiled rice or crusty rolls, and green salad.*

NUTRITION

CALORIES PER PORTION: 255
TOTAL FAT PER PORTION: 10.5 g
SATURATED FAT PER PORTION: 2.5 g

PROTEIN: ★★★ FIBRE: ★ CARBOHYDRATE: ★
VITAMINS: B_3, B_6
MINERALS: K

Note: This dish contains 104 mg cholesterol per portion.

Creamy Thai Chicken Curry

SERVES 4

COCONUT is the only plant high in saturated fat. Some experts believe that the type of saturated fat it contains is *not* bad for us, but until this is confirmed it's wise to limit the amount you eat. This Thai-style curry is just about as healthy a Thai-style curry as you'll get! (It's not too fierce, either.)

1 tablespoon groundnut oil	2 fresh red chillies, deseeded and chopped
4 chicken breast fillets, skinned and each cut into 4	2 large tomatoes, chopped
	2 tablespoons thick canned coconut milk (see note)
1 medium/large onion, finely chopped	
4 cloves garlic, peeled and crushed	4 tablespoons water
2 teaspoons ground cumin	salt and freshly ground black pepper
1 teaspoon garam masala	dash of lime juice
1 teaspoon paprika	2 tablespoons low-fat Greek yogurt

Heat the oil in a non-stick frying pan, add the chicken pieces, and cook over a high heat until brown. Remove the chicken from the pan with a slotted spatula.

Add the onion to the pan, and stir-fry until soft and just turning golden. Add the garlic and dry spices, and stir-fry for 1 minute, then add the chillies, tomatoes and coconut milk, and cook for a further minute.

Return the chicken to the pan with 4 tablespoons water, a little salt and pepper and the lime juice. Simmer for about 15 minutes or until the chicken is tender and the sauce looks good. Stir in the yogurt before serving.

NOTES AND TIPS

✦ *Serve with lots of Thai fragrant rice, (available from larger supermarkets), or plain basmati rice, and salad.*

✦ *You can freeze this dish.*

✦ *When you buy a can of coconut milk and open it, the thicker, creamy coconut milk will have risen to the top. For thick coconut milk, spoon this off (2 tablespoons for this recipe). For thinner coconut milk, stir the contents of the can before using.*

NUTRITION

CALORIES PER PORTION: 250	PROTEIN: ★★★ FIBRE: ★ CARBOHYDRATE: ★
TOTAL FAT PER PORTION: 11 g	VITAMINS: B_3, B_6, beta-carotene, C, E
SATURATED FAT PER PORTION: 4.5 g	MINERALS: K

CHAPTER 6

FISH AND SEAFOOD

In the 1970s and 1980s, we fell out of love with fish in such a big way that most of the high-street fishmongers disappeared, and what fish you could find in the supermarkets was in the frozen-food display, mostly covered in batter. Now you can buy decent fresh fish everywhere, and I love choosing from the ranks of tilapia, skate, John Dory, mullet, bream, bass, pollock, megrim, tuna and dozens more. The point is that fish is not just one taste, as some people think, nor is it bland, as others believe. It can be delicate, strong, meaty, sweet, salty – whatever you want.

Add to the ranks of fish the ever-growing variety of prawns, crabs, lobster, mussels, scallops, and so on, that you can buy, and it's no wonder that there is now more interest in fish and shellfish cookery than ever before. Which is good news for your healthy diet. *All* fish, whether the very low-fat white varieties or the higher-fat oily types, can be eaten as often as you like. Shellfish are low in fat and high in protein, and a good regular addition to your diet, unless you are following a low-cholesterol plan, in which case you should go easy on the crustaceans such as lobster and prawns.

Whatever fish you choose, and however you choose to cook it, try to include it in your diet at least once or twice a week.

Easy Ways to Tasty Fish

When time is short, fish is an ideal food as it is quick to cook. In fact, overcooking is the worst thing you can do to the flavour and texture of fish. Try these quick ideas:

✦ A really fresh whole fish – trout, salmon trout, bass or bream, for instance – needs nothing more than baking in foil, or pan-frying in a very little oil with black pepper, lemon juice, a dash of salt and a dash of white wine.

✦ Meaty fish steaks of cod, swordfish, halibut or monkfish can be grilled or baked with a crust of garlic purée and dried chilli flakes.

✦ Delicate fish, like plaice, turbot and lemon sole, can be cooked *en papillote* – in individual parcels with fresh herbs, julienne vegetables and citrus juice or wine.

Fish Stock

It's hard to buy good fish stock, so it's best to make your own. Save or beg fish heads and bones, and simmer them in water with onion, celery, leek, carrot, a bouquet garni and white peppercorns for 30 minutes. Strain, reduce if you like, and put in the fridge where it will keep for a day or two. Alternatively, the stock can be frozen for a few weeks.

Nutrition Notes

As long as you don't cook fish with too much butter, or add too much extra fat in the form of deep-frying in batter or by adding fatty sauces, everyone, even slimmers, can eat most fish and shellfish without guilt. The oily fishes – mackerel, herring and salmon – are higher in calories because they contain more fat, but this fat is the extremely 'good for you' kind. Officially called 'long chain n-3 fatty acids', they're usually known as 'omega-3s'. This special fat helps ward off heart disease and strokes by lowering the blood's clotting capacity. Because of this, even weight-watchers should eat oily fish regularly – a mackerel or salmon fillet costs no more calories than a small steak.

WHITE FISH Most white fish has a similar nutritional profile, though counts may vary slightly. All are a good, low-fat source of protein and some B vitamins, plus potassium.

Cod per 100 g (3½ oz): 76 calories; a mere 0.5 g fatty acids (20 per cent saturated, 20 per cent mono-unsaturated, 60 per cent polyunsaturated); 46 mg cholesterol; Potassium 320 mg; Magnesium 23 mg; Iron 0.3 mg; Zinc 0.4 mg; vitamin E 0.44 mg; vitamin B_3 1.7 mg; vitamin B_6 0.33 mg; vitamin B_{12} 2 mg.

OILY FISH These are a good source of omega-3s (see list below) and you should try to eat at least one or two portions a week. The most popular oily fish is salmon.

Salmon per 100 g (3½ oz): 182 calories; fatty acids 10.7 g (saturated 20.5 per cent, mono-unsaturated 47.5 per cent, polyunsaturated (including omega-3s) 32 per cent; Cholesterol 50 mg; Potassium 310 mg; Calcium 27 mg; Magnesium 26 mg; Iron 0.7 mg; Zinc 0.8 mg; good source of vitamins B_1, B_3, B_6, B_{12} and folic acid.

SOURCES OF OMEGA-3S

Per 100 g (3½ oz) fish: Mackerel 2.5 g; Herring 1.6 g; Mullet 1.1 g; Salmon 1.0 g; Halibut 0.9 g; Rainbow trout 0.5 g; Tuna 0.5 g.

SHELLFISH These are a good source of protein and minerals.

Prawns, shelled, per 100 g (3½ oz): 107 calories; fatty acids 1.3 g (saturated 31 per cent, mono-unsaturated 38.5 per cent, polyunsaturated 30.5 per cent); Cholesterol 81 mg; Potassium 260 mg; Calcium 150 mg; Magnesium 42 mg; Iron 1.1 mg; Zinc 1.6 mg.

CALORIE AND FAT COUNTS FOR FISH AND SHELLFISH

Fresh raw fish, filleted, per 25 g (1 oz)

White fish	Cals	Fat (grams)
Cod, coley	19	0.2
Haddock, monkfish	18	0.15
Halibut, plaice	23	0.6
Skate	25	0.25
Sole	20	0.3
Swordfish, bass, mullet, bream	31	1.2
Oily fish		
Herring	60	5.0
Herring roes	26	0.5
Kipper	52	3.0
Mackerel	57	4.0
Salmon, fresh	46	3.0
Salmon, smoked	42	2.5
Sardines, fresh	45	2.3
Trout	35	1.1
Tuna, fresh	35	1.5

Shellfish, per 25 g (1 oz), flesh only

	Cals	Fat (grams)
Crab	32	1.3
Lobster	30	1.0
Mussels	22	0.5
Oysters	13	0.2
Prawns	27	0.3
Scallops	27	0.3
Squid	20	0.3

Canned fish, per 25 g (1 oz)

	Cals	Fat (grams)
Anchovies, drained	67	5.0
Pilchard in tomato sauce	32	1.4
Sardines in oil, drained	55	3.5
Salmon, red	44	2.3
Tuna in brine, drained	25	0.2
Tuna in oil, drained	48	2.3

Miscellaneous

	Cals	Fat (grams)
Caviar, per 25 g (1 oz)	65	3.7
Fish and chips, traditional, average portion	1000	50.0
Whitebait, deep-fried, per 25 g (1 oz)	135	12.0

Salmon Skewers with Hot Sauce and Avocado

SERVES 4

THIS dish is high in vitamin E and the omega-3 oils, but, more importantly, it tastes terrific and, if you're busy, makes an ideal dinner-party main course for summer, perhaps with a chilled soup starter and a fresh fruit dessert.

4 thick salmon fillets, each weighing about 140 g (5 oz)	200 g (7 oz) low-fat Greek yogurt
1 teaspoon Cajun seasoning	6.5 cm (2½ inch) piece of cucumber, finely chopped
salt and freshly ground black pepper	1 medium ripe avocado
juice of 2 limes	225 g (8 oz) easy-cook mixed white long-grain and wild rice
1 fresh green chilli, deseeded and finely chopped	1 tablespoon light olive oil
handful of fresh coriander or dill leaf, chopped	

Cut the salmon into 2.5 cm (1 inch) cubes. Sprinkle the Cajun seasoning, some black pepper and half the lime juice into a shallow bowl, add the salmon and coat thoroughly with the mixture. Cover and leave for 30 minutes if possible.

Meanwhile, to make the sauce, mix the chilli and coriander or dill with the yogurt and cucumber, and keep cool.

Halve, stone, peel and slice the avocado and immediately coat it with the remainder of the lime juice. Cook the rice in lightly salted boiling water for the recommended cooking time (about 20 minutes). About 10 minutes before the rice is ready, preheat the grill and thread the salmon on to four small skewers. Brush the salmon with the olive oil, and grill under a medium hot heat for about 3 minutes, then turn, brush with oil again, and grill for a further 2–3 minutes. Baste during grilling with anything that remains of the spice marinade.

Arrange the avocado on four serving plates. When the rice is tender, drain and serve it with the salmon skewers and a portion of the sauce next to the avocado.

NOTES AND TIPS
✦ *Don't overcook the salmon or it will be dry.*
✦ *A mixed salad would go well with this dish.*

NUTRITION

CALORIES PER PORTION: 560
TOTAL FAT PER PORTION: 28 g
SATURATED FAT PER PORTION: 7 g

PROTEIN: ★★★ FIBRE: ★ CARBOHYDRATE: ★★
VITAMINS: B₃, E
MINERALS: K, Zn, Ca, Mg

Salmon Fishcakes

SERVES 4

THE touch of light mayonnaise in these luxury fishcakes makes them really lovely. Made my way, there is no need to fry them – they bake in the oven perfectly well.

500 g (22 oz) floury potatoes	1 medium red pepper, deseeded and finely chopped
Salt and freshly ground black pepper	
400 g (14 oz) salmon fillet	1 tablespoon reduced-fat mayonnaise
100 ml (3½ fl oz), plus 1 tablespoon skimmed milk	1 size-3 egg, beaten
	2 teaspoons plain flour
25 g (1 oz) low-fat spread	6.5 cm (2½ inch) piece of cucumber
4 tablespoons stale breadcrumbs	4 tablespoons low-fat natural Bio yogurt

Peel the potatoes, cut them into chunks and cook in lightly salted boiling water until tender. Meanwhile, put the salmon in a frying pan with the 100 ml (3½ oz) milk, season with a little salt and pepper, and poach for about 8 minutes or until barely cooked.

While the salmon and potatoes are cooking, heat the low-fat spread in a small frying pan, add the breadcrumbs and stir-fry until lightly golden and all the spread is absorbed. Soften the red pepper in a little water in a small saucepan (or in a bowl with a little water, covered, in the microwave for 2 minutes on high), and drain.

Drain the salmon, reserving the cooking milk, and flake the salmon. Drain the potatoes and mash with 2–3 tablespoons of the salmon milk, the mayonnaise and half the egg. Season with salt and pepper, add the flaked salmon and the red pepper, and mix gently (do not use a blender or processor).

Flour your hands and form the mixture into eight patties (they will be quite soft, but don't worry). Mix the remainder of the egg with the remaining 1 tablespoon milk, and coat the patties with this egg mixture, then dip them in the breadcrumbs.

Place on a baking tray and bake the fishcakes in the oven at 190°C/375°F/Gas Mark 5 for 15 minutes or until golden.

Meanwhile, to make the sauce, finely chop the cucumber and mix with the yogurt. Serve the fish cakes with the sauce.

NOTES AND TIPS

✦ *You can substitute finely chopped fresh parsley for the red pepper if you like.*
✦ *Serve the fishcakes with a large green salad.*

NUTRITION

CALORIES PER PORTION (2 FISHCAKES): 340
TOTAL FAT PER PORTION: 17.5 g
SATURATED FAT PER PORTION: 4.5 g

PROTEIN: ★★★ FIBRE: ★★ CARBOHYDRATE: ★★
VITAMINS: B group, C, A, D, E, beta-carotene
MINERALS: K, Zn, Ca, Mg, Fe

Note: This dish contains 113 mg cholesterol per portion.

Chilli Barbecued Monkfish with Herb Couscous

SERVES 4

IF YOU haven't given couscous a try yet, do. It is light, and makes a pleasant change from rice with all spicy dishes, such as this one. In fact, it's better than rice because it 'soaks up' the flavours very well. The barbecue seasoning originates from Morocco and is called a *chermoula*.

800 g (1¾ lb) monkfish fillet, cubed	1 teaspoon ground saffron
2 large cloves garlic, peeled and finely chopped	juice of 1 lemon
1 red onion, finely chopped	2 tablespoons olive oil
small bunch of flat-leafed parsley, finely chopped	salt and freshly ground black pepper
1 heaped teaspoon ground coriander	225 g (8 oz) couscous
1 heaped teaspoon ground paprika	handful of fresh coriander leaves, chopped
1 teaspoon dried chilli flakes	

Put the fish in a shallow bowl. Mix together all the remaining ingredients, except the couscous and fresh coriander, and coat the fish well with this mixture. Leave to marinate for 30 minutes.

Soak the couscous according to packet instructions and put in a steamer or colander over a pan of boiling water to heat through.

Thread the fish on to skewers and cook under a hot grill for 6–7 minutes, turning once and basting with the marinade. Fluff up the couscous with a fork before serving, and stir in the coriander. Serve the fish on the couscous.

NOTES AND TIPS

✦ *Read the couscous packet instructions carefully as they do vary.*
✦ *You can make this dish with any firm fish, such as fresh tuna, swordfish or even cod.*

NUTRITION

CALORIES PER PORTION: 440   PROTEIN: ★★★ FIBRE: ★★ CARBOHYDRATE: ★★
TOTAL FAT PER PORTION: 10 g   VITAMINS: B₃, C, E
SATURATED FAT PER PORTION: 1.5 g   MINERALS: K, Zn, Ca
Note: This dish contains 92 mg cholesterol per portion.

Crunchy Seafood Gratin

SERVES 4

CRISPY bread makes a nice change from pastry, potato or savoury crumble as a topping for all kinds of bakes and gratins. Saving fat on the topping means that you can use some cream in the sauce, and still have a very low-calorie main course!

3 slices of stale wholemeal bread, crusts removed	400 g (14 oz) frozen mixed seafood, thawed (see note)
2 teaspoons groundnut oil	pinch of seafood seasoning
2 leeks, sliced	40 g (1½ oz) low-fat spread
1 clove garlic, peeled and lightly bruised	40 g (1½ oz) plain flour
700 ml (1¼ pints) skimmed milk	1 teaspoon lemon juice
salt and freshly ground black pepper	1 teaspoon mustard powder
200 g (7 oz) haddock, cod or coley fillet, skinned	2 tablespoons half-fat cream
100 g (3½ oz) small mushrooms, halved	2 tablespoons grated half-fat Cheddar-style cheese

Shred the bread on a coarse grater or simply chop into small pieces. Heat the oil in a non-stick frying pan and, over a very high heat, stir-fry the leeks and garlic for 1 minute. Remove with a slotted spoon to a plate. Add the bread to the pan and stir for 1 minute. (There will be hardly any oil left in the pan when you do this, but it doesn't matter.) When the bread is just taking on a darker colour, remove from the pan and set aside.

Put the milk in the frying pan, season with salt and pepper, and add the fish, leeks, garlic and mushrooms. Poach gently for 10 minutes, then add the mixed seafood and cook for a further 1–2 minutes. Strain the milk off the pan and into a jug, then flake the fish and arrange it, with the seafood, leeks and mushrooms (discard the garlic) in a large gratin dish. Sprinkle the seafood seasoning over and keep warm.

Melt the low-fat spread in a saucepan and add the flour. Stir for 1 minute, then gradually add the poaching milk, stirring all the time. When you have a smooth sauce, stir in the lemon juice, mustard and cream, check the seasoning and pour over the fish and vegetables. Sprinkle the bread, and then the cheese, on top and put under a medium grill for 4–5 minutes to heat through and brown the topping.

NOTES AND TIPS

✦ *Mixed seafood is available in 400 g (14 oz) packs in the frozen food cabinet of most supermarkets. Thaw thoroughly.*

✦ *Serve a mixed salad, or broccoli and peas with this dish.*

NUTRITION

CALORIES PER PORTION: **365**	PROTEIN: ★★★ FIBRE: ★★ CARBOHYDRATE: ★★
TOTAL FAT PER PORTION: **12 g**	VITAMINS: **B group**
SATURATED FAT PER PORTION: **3.5 g**	MINERALS: **K, Mg, Ca, Zn, Fe**

Note: This recipe contains 95 mg cholesterol and 1324 mg sodium per portion.

English Cod and Prawn Pie

SERVES 4

THIS dish was one of my childhood favourites, but made, in those days, with full cream milk, lots of butter, full-fat cheese and tons of fat in the topping. In the health–conscious 1990s, this version is a better bet – and just as nice.

725 ml (26 fl oz) skimmed milk	2 teaspoons lemon juice
salt and freshly ground black pepper	110 g (4 oz) half-fat Cheddar-style cheese, grated
450 g (1 lb) cod fillet	
675 g (1½ lb) old potatoes	100 g (3½ oz) small mushrooms, sliced
2 tablespoons 70 per cent fat-free mayonnaise	175 g (6 oz) cooked peeled prawns
200 g (7 oz) broccoli florets	good handful of fresh parsley, chopped
40 g (1½ oz) low-fat spread	1 tablespoon grated half-fat mozzarella or Cheddar-style cheese
40 g (1½ oz) plain flour	
1 teaspoon mustard powder	

Put 700 ml (1¼ pints) milk in a frying pan, season with salt and pepper, add the cod and poach gently until just tender. Drain the fish, reserving the poaching milk. Break the fish into big flakes and place in a shallow ovenproof casserole. Preheat the oven to 170°C/375°F/Gas Mark 5.

Peel and chop the potatoes, and cook in lightly salted boiling water until tender. Drain and mash with the remaining 25 ml (1 fl oz) skimmed milk and the mayonnaise. Parboil or microwave the broccoli.

Meanwhile, to make the cheese sauce, melt the low–fat spread in a small saucepan and stir in the flour. Cook for 1 minute, stirring, then gradually add the reserved poaching milk, stirring, until you have a smooth sauce. Add the mustard, lemon juice and Cheddar cheese, and stir to melt. Check the seasoning.

Arrange the broccoli, mushrooms, prawns and parsley on top of the cod, then pour the cheese sauce over. Pipe or spoon the mashed potato around the edge of the pie and across the middle. Sprinkle the mozzarella or Cheddar cheese over the sauce that is still showing, and bake in the oven for 30 minutes or until the sauce and potatoes are golden.

NOTES AND TIPS
+ *Serve with sweetcorn and peas to add plenty of fibre.*
+ *Use coley, haddock or monkfish instead of cod if you like.*

NUTRITION

CALORIES PER PORTION: 520 PROTEIN: ★★★ FIBRE: ★★ CARBOHYDRATE: ★★
TOTAL FAT PER PORTION: 12 g VITAMINS: B group, C, E, beta-carotene
SATURATED FAT PER PORTION: 5 g MINERALS: K, Ca, Mg, Zn
Note: This dish contains 161 mg cholesterol per portion.

Scampi Provençal

SERVES 4

COOKED well, this is one of my favourite very low-fat, high-taste, quick meals.

1½ tablespoons olive oil	125 ml (4½ fl oz) dry white wine
1 medium onion, finely chopped	1 teaspoon crushed dried chillies
2 cloves garlic, peeled and finely chopped	1 bay leaf
450 g (1 lb) raw scampi, peeled (see note)	freshly ground black pepper
400 g (14 oz) can chopped tomatoes with herbs	good handful of flat-leafed parsley, roughly chopped, to garnish

Heat half the oil in a non-stick frying pan, add the onion and garlic, and sauté until soft and just turning golden. Remove the onion with a slotted spoon and reserve.

Add the rest of the oil to the pan and, over a medium heat, cook the scampi for 1–2 minutes. Remove from the pan and set aside.

Return the onions to the pan and add the rest of the ingredients, except the parsley. Simmer for 30 minutes. Put the scampi back into the pan and simmer for 2 minutes to heat through. Serve garnished with parsley.

NOTES AND TIPS

✦ *If you can get real scampi (langoustines) for this dish, so much the better, but any large, firm prawns will do. However, those midget frozen prawns just aren't substantial enough for this dish. You can use cooked prawns if you can't get them raw, but there's no need to fry them; simply add them to the dish and heat through just before serving.*

✦ *To cut the cost of this dish you could substitute half the scampi with firm white fish, cut into cubes. Pre-fry with the scampi, and return to the pan a few minutes before the scampi at the end of the simmering time.*

✦ *Serve this dish with plenty of rice and salad.*

NUTRITION

CALORIES PER PORTION: 225	PROTEIN: ★★★ FIBRE: ★ CARBOHYDRATE: ★
TOTAL FAT PER PORTION: 8 g	VITAMINS: beta-carotene, C, E
SATURATED FAT PER PORTION: 1 g	MINERALS: Zn, K, Ca, Mg

Note: This dish contains 225 mg cholesterol and about 1800 mg sodium per portion.

Salmon and Broccoli Pancakes

SERVES 4

I THINK pancakes are a very underrated food in savoury dishes. Filled with a creamy sauce and salmon or chicken with vegetables, they make a mouthwatering meal for all the family.

375 g (12 oz) salmon fillet	2 tablespoons grated half-fat Cheddar-style cheese
700 ml (1¼ pints) skimmed milk	
1 small onion, halved	**For the pancakes**
salt and freshly ground black pepper	110 g (4 oz) wholemeal flour
200 g (7 oz) broccoli florets	salt and freshly ground pepper
40 g (1½ oz) low-fat spread	1 size-3 egg, beaten
40 g (1½ oz) plain flour	250 ml (9 fl oz) skimmed milk
½ teaspoon mustard powder	2 teaspoons corn oil

Put the salmon in a frying pan with the skimmed milk and onion. Season with salt and pepper, and poach for a few minutes or until barely cooked. Drain, reserving the milk, and flake the salmon. Discard the onion. Parboil the broccoli, drain and reserve.

Melt the low-fat spread in a saucepan, stir in the flour, and cook, stirring, for 1 minute, then gradually add the reserved poaching milk, stirring all the time. Finally, add the mustard and check the seasoning. Stir in the salmon and broccoli. Keep warm.

To make the pancakes, sift the flour and a little salt into a mixing bowl, make a well in the centre and add the beaten egg. Gradually beat the egg and flour together, and finally add the milk, beating until you have a smooth batter.

Brush a small, good-quality non-stick frying pan (preferably used only for omelettes and pancakes) with a little of the oil, and heat until the pan is very hot. Add about one eighth of the pancake batter to the pan, swirling it around to coat the bottom thinly and evenly. Cook for 1 minute, lifting up the edge to make sure the underside of the pancake is golden, and then turn, using a long spatula, and cook the other side for a few seconds. Remove to a plate and keep warm. Cook seven more pancakes in this way. Fill each pancake when it is cooked with one eighth of the salmon and broccoli mixture, and place side by side in an oblong, shallow ovenproof dish.

When all the pancakes are in the dish, sprinkle the cheese over the top and pop the dish under a medium hot grill for a few minutes to heat the pancakes through again and to brown the cheese.

NOTES AND TIPS

✦ *Serve the pancakes with new potatoes and asparagus tips or mangetout.*

NUTRITION

CALORIES PER PORTION: 490	PROTEIN: ★★★ FIBRE: ★★ CARBOHYDRATE: ★★
TOTAL FAT PER PORTION: 21 g	VITAMINS: A, B group, D, E
SATURATED FAT PER PORTION: 5 g	MINERALS: K, Ca, Mg, Zn, Fe

Note: This recipe contains 117 mg cholesterol per portion.

Monkfish, Prawn and Red Pepper Stir-Fry

SERVES 4

MORE and more good-quality prawns are appearing in our supermarkets and on our fish stalls. If you can get tiger prawns for this dish, so much the better, but any large, firm prawns will do. If you can get them raw, better still.

1½ tablespoons sesame or groundnut oil	8 spring onions, trimmed and halved lengthways
2 cloves garlic, peeled and chopped	
1 large fresh red chilli, deseeded and chopped	1 tablespoon white wine vinegar
1 knob of fresh root ginger, peeled and chopped	1 teaspoon runny honey
	1 tablespoon light soy sauce
300 g (11 oz) monkfish fillet, cubed	2 teaspoons plum sauce (see note)
1 medium red pepper, deseeded and sliced	100 g (3½ oz) beansprouts
50 g (2 oz) mangetout	fresh coriander leaves, to garnish
225 g (8 oz) tiger prawns, peeled	

Heat the oil in a wok, add the garlic, chilli and ginger, and stir-fry over a medium heat for 30 seconds (don't allow the garlic to burn). Add the monkfish, red pepper and mangetout, and the prawns, if raw, and stir-fry for 2 minutes. Add the rest of the ingredients (and the prawns, if cooked), except the coriander, and stir-fry for a further 2 minutes. (Add a little water or fish stock if you like a wetter stir-fry.) Serve, garnished with coriander.

NOTES AND TIPS
✦ *If you haven't got plum sauce, use hoisin sauce instead.*
✦ *This dish is delicious served with Thai fragrant rice or with rice noodles.*
✦ *Any very firm white fish can be used instead of the monkfish – swordfish would be ideal.*

NUTRITION

CALORIES PER PORTION: 200	PROTEIN: ★★★ FIBRE: ★ CARBOHYDRATE: ★
TOTAL FAT PER PORTION: 7.5 g	VITAMINS: E, C, beta-carotene, folic acid, B$_3$
SATURATED FAT PER PORTION: 1.5 g	MINERALS: Zn, Ca, K, Mg

Note: This dish contains 150 mg cholesterol and 1100 mg sodium per portion.

Halibut Steaks with A Crusted Herb Topping

SERVES 4

THIS recipe doesn't take much longer to prepare than plain baked or grilled fish, so why not give it a try?

4 halibut steaks, about 200 g (7 oz) each	handful each of fresh parsley and chives, chopped
2 tablespoons lime juice	1 teaspoon crushed fennel seeds
4 tablespoons wholemeal breadcrumbs	1 clove garlic, peeled and finely chopped
40 g (1½ oz) half-fat Cheddar-style cheese, grated	25 g (1 oz) low-fat spread
½ teaspoon mustard powder	salt and freshly ground black pepper
4 spring onions, finely chopped	

Preheat the oven to 180°C/350°F/Gas Mark 4.

Put the fish steaks in a shallow ovenproof dish in which they fit tightly in one layer. Combine all the other ingredients in a small bowl until you have a thick paste, then spread this evenly over the steaks. Bake in the oven for 20 minutes or until the fish is cooked and the topping is golden.

NOTES AND TIPS

✦ *You could use swordfish or cod steaks instead of the halibut.*

NUTRITION

CALORIES PER PORTION: 230	PROTEIN: ★★★ FIBRE: ★ CARBOHYDRATE: ★
TOTAL FAT PER PORTION: 6 g	VITAMINS: B₃, B₁₂, B₆, E, A
SATURATED FAT PER PORTION: 2 g	MINERALS: K, Mg, Ca

Note: This recipe contains 104 mg cholesterol per portion.

Skate with Vinegar Sauce

SERVES 4

THIS is based on the classic skate in black butter, but this healthier version has all the flavour and delicious piquancy with half the fat. Give it a try – skate is a lovely fish with none of those tiny bones to irritate you, and the dish is simple to cook.

4 good-sized skate wings	2 teaspoons capers, drained (see note)
1 tablespoon seasoned flour	4 tablespoons white wine vinegar
1 tablespoon groundnut oil	sprigs fresh coriander or snipped fresh chives, to garnish
25 g (1 oz) low-salt butter	

Dry the skate on kitchen paper and coat with the seasoned flour. Heat the oil in a large non-stick frying pan (or two smaller ones) and sauté the wings for about 10 minutes or until cooked, turning once. (Overlap the thin ends of the wings so they don't get over-cooked while the thicker ends are cooking.)

When the fish is cooked, remove to a serving plate and keep warm. Wipe the pan out with kitchen paper, return to the hob, add the butter and, over a high heat, melt until it is sizzling and just turning golden. Quickly add the capers and vinegar, and swirl around. Pour over the skate and serve, garnished with herbs.

NUTRITION

CALORIES PER PORTION: 230
TOTAL FAT PER PORTION: 10.5 g
SATURATED FAT PER PORTION: 4 g

PROTEIN: ★★★ FIBRE: ★ CARBOHYDRATE: ★
VITAMINS: E, B$_3$, folic acid
MINERALS: Ca, Mg, K

Note: This recipe contains 101 mg cholesterol per portion.

Tandoori Cod Bake

SERVES 4

AN EASY, very low-fat supper for all who enjoy hot and spicy food. Don't use tandoori *paste* in this dish, though – it's very high in fat.

900 g (2 lb) cod fillet, cut into 2.5 cm (1 inch) cubes	4 shallots, peeled and finely chopped
1 tablespoon tandoori powder (see note)	juice of 1 lemon
250 g (9 oz) low-fat natural Bio yogurt	1 clove garlic, peeled finely chopped
	lemon wedges, to serve

Put the cod in a shallow ovenproof dish. Mix the tandoori powder with the yogurt, shallots, lemon juice and garlic, and pour over the cod to coat it thoroughly. Leave to marinate for 30 minutes.

Preheat the oven to 180°C/350°F/Gas Mark 4, and bake the cod for 20 minutes or until the pieces are cooked through and you have a deep red, fairly dry, slightly charred sauce. Serve at once, with lemon wedges.

NOTES AND TIPS

✦ *You can make your own tandoori powder by mixing 2 teaspoons paprika with 1 teaspoon each of ground coriander, cumin, chilli and ginger.*

✦ *Good accompaniments would be basmati rice, mixed salad, and cucumber and yogurt raita.*

NUTRITION

CALORIES PER PORTION: 210
TOTAL FAT PER PORTION: 2.5 g
SATURATED FAT PER PORTION: 1 g

PROTEIN: ★★★ FIBRE: ★ CARBOHYDRATE: ★
VITAMINS: E, A, C
MINERALS: Ca, K, Mg, Fe

Catalan Tuna Casserole

SERVES 4

FRESH tuna is quite widely available now. Not only is it deliciously meaty but it also contains those good-for-you omega-3 fish oils. This simple casserole, based on one you'll find in rural Spain, is ideal for a one-pot family meal, and for slimmers.

1½ tablespoons olive oil	100 ml (3½ fl oz) fish stock
4 fresh tuna steaks, each weighing about 175 g (6 oz), floured	1 medium green pepper, deseeded and chopped into 1 cm (½ inch) pieces
1 Spanish onion, finely chopped	125 ml (4½ fl oz) dry white wine
2 cloves garlic, peeled and crushed	2 teaspoons lemon juice
450 g (1 lb) waxy potatoes, peeled and chopped into 1 cm (½ inch) pieces	1 bay leaf
400 g (14 oz) can plum tomatoes	50 g (2 oz) mushrooms
1 tablespoon tomato purée	salt and freshly ground black pepper

Heat half the olive oil in a flameproof casserole, add the tuna steaks and cook quickly on both sides over a high heat until browned. Remove the tuna from the pan, and clean the pan.

Heat the rest of the oil in the casserole, add the onion and garlic, and stir-fry over a medium heat until soft. Meanwhile, parboil the potatoes for 5 minutes, and drain. Add the potatoes, tomatoes with their juice, tomato purée, fish stock and green pepper to the casserole, cover and simmer for 20 minutes.

Add the tuna steaks, wine, lemon juice, bay leaf and mushrooms, and season with salt and pepper. Make sure the tuna is well buried in the sauce. Cover and simmer gently for 20 minutes or until the tuna is tender and you have a good rich sauce.

NOTES AND TIPS
+ *Serve with salad or just on its own.*
+ *You can use other, firm-fleshed fish for this dish, such as swordfish.*

NUTRITION

CALORIES PER PORTION: 440　　PROTEIN: ★★★ FIBRE: ★★ CARBOHYDRATE: ★★
TOTAL FAT PER PORTION: 21 g　　VITAMINS: B group, C, E, beta-carotene
SATURATED FAT PER PORTION: 3 g　　MINERALS: K, Zn

Swordfish Steaks with Saffron Sauce

SERVES 4

I LOVE saffron dearly; it doesn't only give a perfect lemon yellow colour but also a taste you can't copy. Turmeric just won't do! One 0.4 g sachet of saffron strands is plenty for this dish.

1 sachet saffron strands	250 ml (9 fl oz) fish stock (see note)
25 ml (1 fl oz) boiling water	salt and freshly ground black pepper
2 teaspoons olive oil	1 tablespoon dry sherry
15 g (½ oz) butter	4 tablespoons half-fat cream
1 small onion, very finely chopped	chopped fresh parsley, to garnish
1 clove garlic, peeled and chopped	
4 swordfish steaks, each weighing about 200 g (7 oz)	

Steep the saffron in the boiling water for 10 minutes. Meanwhile, heat the oil and butter in a large non-stick frying pan, add the onion and garlic, and stir-fry for a few minutes or until soft.

Push the onion to the edges of the pan and turn the heat up a little. Add the swordfish to the centre of the pan and seal on either side, until slightly golden. Add the stock and saffron infusion, season with salt and pepper, and turn down the heat. Simmer for 8 minutes or until the steaks are just cooked.

Remove the fish to serving plates and keep warm. Strain the cooking liquid and return to the pan with the sherry. Bubble for a few minutes to reduce to a thin sauce, then turn the heat off and stir in the cream. Serve the fish with the sauce poured around or over, and garnished with parsley.

NOTES AND TIPS

✦ *To make a fish stock, find a fishmonger who will give you the bones, heads, etc, of a few fish. Simmer them in water in a saucepan with some onion, celery, leek, carrot and peppercorns, and some fresh thyme, for 30 minutes, then strain. If you have to buy commercial fish stock you will probably not need to add any salt to this dish, so do taste before seasoning.*

✦ *As this fish dish is low in fibre, add plenty of new potatoes, broccoli and green beans for a complete balanced meal.*

NUTRITION

CALORIES PER PORTION: 265	PROTEIN: ★★★ FIBRE: ★ CARBOHYDRATE: ★
TOTAL FAT PER PORTION: 12.5 g	VITAMINS: B_3, folic acid, A
SATURATED FAT PER PORTION: 3.5 g	MINERALS: K, Mg, Ca

CHAPTER 7

VEGETARIAN DISHES

A vegetarian, or demi-vegetarian, diet wins more converts every year. Many people who give up meat do so hoping that it will help them to become more healthy, and it is true that a carefully thought out, varied vegetarian diet can be very healthy, but it does take a little know-how; it is quite easy, unless you're careful, to eat *more* saturated fat and overall fat than meat-eaters, and it is possible to fall short of some nutrients if your diet is too restricted. The guidelines on healthy eating (see pages 8–18) also apply to vegetarians, but the tips below will help you to plan out your diet.

I hope the recipes in this chapter will give you some inspiration. Also, many of the soups, starters and snacks (pages 28–40) are vegetarian, as are several of the salads (pages 120–131), pasta and grain recipes (pages 104–119), and all the desserts. Even some of the meat, fish and poultry recipes can be adapted to be cooked using soya meat substitutes, tofu chunks or Quorn. For example, you could use tofu in the Monkfish, Prawn and Red Pepper Stir-Fry (page 85), or Quorn in the Creamy Thai Chicken Curry (page 74).

Nutrition Notes

If you are following a completely vegetarian diet, the main points to watch are:

✦ Don't just give up meat and not replace it with another protein source in your diet.

✦ Don't always pick dairy produce as your replacement protein source. Full-fat dairy produce, such as Cheddar cheese, full-cream milk, and eggs, are high in saturated fat and eggs are high in cholesterol (250 mg each), so should be limited if you are following a low-cholesterol diet. Non-dairy sources of protein, none of which are high in saturates, are: all pulses, e.g. lentils, chickpeas, dried beans of all kinds, and their canned equivalents; soya products, such as TVP mince and tofu; Quorn. Nuts and seeds also contain good amounts of protein, as do several carbohydrate foods, such as potatoes, rice, pasta and most grains. Even some vegetables, such as cauliflower, leeks and spinach, contain protein. Mixing the different types of non-dairy protein at each meal is the ideal, e.g. a grain with a pulse, or a pulse with nuts or seeds. When you do eat dairy produce, try to use the lower-fat versions.

◆ Ensure your diet is varied.

◆ Eat plenty of fresh fruits and vegetables, especially green, leafy vegetables.

◆ Lastly, be sure to also read the first chapter of this book on healthy eating.

CALORIE AND FAT COUNTS FOR VEGETARIAN FOODS

Eggs and cheese, per 25 g (1 oz) unless otherwise stated (for other dairy products, see page 134)

	Cals	Fat (grams)
Egg, size 3, one, raw or cooked without fat	80	6.0
Brie or Camembert	75	5.8
Cheddar	101	8.3
Cheddar-style, half-fat	62	3.5
Cottage cheese	24	1.0
Cream cheese, full-fat	110	12.0
Danish Blue	89	7.3
Dolcelatte	94	7.5
Edam	76	5.7
Mozzarella	62	4.7
Mozzarella, half-fat	45	2.6
Soft cheese, low-fat	33	2.1
Stilton	115	10.0

Vegetable proteins, per 25 g (1 oz)

Quorn	21	0.8
Tofu	17	1.0
TVP mince or chunks, when reconstituted with water	17	trace

Pulses, per 25 g (1 oz), all cooked weights

Baked beans in tomato sauce	16	trace
Butter beans, haricot beans	23	trace
Chickpeas	40	0.8
Black-eye	29	trace
Borlotti, cannellini, flageolet	20	trace
Kidney beans, lentils	25	trace

Nuts and seeds, per 25 g (1 oz), all shelled weight

Almonds	141	13.3
Brazils	155	15.3
Chestnuts	42	0.7

	Cals	Fat (grams)
Hazelnuts	95	9.0
Peanuts, fresh	142	12.2
Pine nuts	172	17.0
Walnuts	131	9.0
Sesame seeds	150	14.5
Sunflower seeds	145	12.0

Carbohydrates, per 25 g (1 oz)

Bread, white	59	0.5
Bread, wholemeal	55	0.5
Flour, white	85	0.3
Flour, wholemeal	77	0.5
Potato, plain cooked	20	trace
Sweet potato	22	trace
Parsnip, plainly cooked	16	0.3

(For rice and pasta, see pages 105–106.)

Vegetables, raw or plainly cooked, per 25 g (1 oz)

Aubergine	3.5	trace
Beans, French	10	trace
Beans, runner	5	trace
Broccoli	6	0.2
Brussels sprouts	9	0.3
Cabbage, most kinds	5	trace
Carrots	6	trace
Cauliflower	7	0.2
Courgettes	5	trace
Leek	6	trace
Mushrooms	3	trace
Onion	9	trace
Peas	20	0.4
Pumpkin, peeled	3	trace
Spinach and spring greens	6	0.2
Swede and turnip	6	trace
Sweetcorn kernels	30	0.5
Squash, butternut	9	trace
Tomatoes, 400 g (14 oz) can	64	0.4

(For salad vegetables, see page 121.)

Imam Bayeldi (Stuffed Aubergines)

SERVES 4

AUBERGINES are very low in calories, yet high in fibre, filling and satisfying. I used to cook this Turkish dish with masses of oil because aubergines act like thirsty sponges when you pre-fry them. But they taste just as good simply brushed lightly with oil and baked or grilled. This is a light dish — good for a lunch with pittas, or, if you are ravenous, as a starter. Or perhaps you could eat two . . .

2 large aubergines	400 g (14 oz) can plum tomatoes
salt and freshly ground black pepper	1 teaspoon dark brown sugar
1½ tablespoons olive oil	½ teaspoon ground allspice
1 medium onion, finely chopped	2 tablespoons chopped fresh parsley
1 large green pepper, deseeded and finely chopped	250 ml (9 fl oz) tomato juice
1 clove garlic, peeled and finely chopped	fresh coriander leaves, to garnish
50 g (2 oz) sultanas	

Slice the aubergines in half lengthways, scoop out half the flesh and reserve. Sprinkle salt on the insides of the aubergine halves and leave, skin-side up, for 1 hour. Meanwhile, chop the reserved aubergine flesh. Heat 1 tablespoon oil in a frying pan, add the onion, green pepper and garlic, and sauté until soft and turning golden. Add the aubergine flesh and cook for 1–2 minutes, then add the sultanas, tomatoes (roughly broken up) with their juice, the sugar, allspice and parsley. Season with salt and pepper, and simmer for 30 minutes or until you have a rich mixture.

Rinse and dry the aubergine cases and rub the rest of the oil all over the skin and flesh, then place the cases in a suitable baking dish with the tomato juice poured around them. Fill the cases with the onion mixture, cover, and bake in the oven at 190°C/375°F/Gas Mark 5 for about 45 minutes. Serve garnished with coriander leaves.

NOTES AND TIPS

✦ *A quicker, similar type of recipe would be to make the filling as above but just to chop the aubergines and add them to the pan with the tomatoes. You would then have a tasty one-pan supper instead, ideal with crusty bread.*

NUTRITION

CALORIES PER PORTION: 150	PROTEIN: ★ FIBRE: ★★ CARBOHYDRATE: ★★★
TOTAL FAT PER PORTION: 6.5 g	VITAMINS: beta-carotene, C, E
SATURATED FAT PER PORTION: 1 g	MINERALS: K, Zn, Fe

Mixed Pepper Tortilla

SERVES 4

AS LONG as you. don't rely on egg meals too much if you're trying to eat more vegetarian dishes, an occasional egg supper is a good idea. Eggs are vitamin–and iron-rich, and a vegetable tortilla is a great way to serve them.

6 size-3 eggs	1 large leek, sliced
salt and freshly ground black pepper	1 red, 1 yellow and 1 green pepper, deseeded and sliced
75 ml (3 fl oz) skimmed milk	
1½ tablespoons olive oil	400 g (14 oz) old potatoes, peeled and boiled

Beat the eggs in a bowl with the seasoning and milk. Heat the oil in a large non-stick frying pan, add the leek and peppers, and stir-fry for about 15 minutes or until soft. Slice the potatoes and arrange over the pepper mixture to cover the whole pan area. Pour the egg mixture over evenly and cook on a low to medium heat for about 10 minutes or until the underside is golden. Flash the tortilla under a grill (still in the pan) to brown the top, and then invert on to a serving platter and slice into wedges. Eat warm or cold.

NOTES AND TIPS

◆ *The tortilla is nice served with hunks of bread and a little salad.*

◆ *Pack a wedge of tortilla in a lunchbox instead of a slice of far-more-fattening quiche.*

◆ *Try other combinations of vegetables, e.g. courgettes and sweetcorn.*

NUTRITION

CALORIES PER PORTION: 285	PROTEIN: ★★★ FIBRE: ★★ CARBOHYDRATE: ★★
TOTAL FAT PER PORTION: 15 g	VITAMINS: A, B group, D, C, E, beta-carotene
SATURATED FAT PER PORTION: 4 g	MINERALS: Fe, K, Ca

Note: This dish contains 375 mg cholesterol per portion.

Three-Mushroom Risotto

SERVES 4

A NICE, creamy mushroom risotto is certainly one of my favourite things. It's one of those perfect meals that has all the right things in all the right proportions – high carbohydrates, medium protein and low saturated fats.

25 g (1 oz) dried *porcini* mushrooms	150 g (5½ oz) shiitake mushrooms
140 ml (¼ pint) water	300 g (11 oz) Arborio rice
825 ml (1½ pints) vegetable stock	salt and freshly ground black pepper
25 g (1 oz) butter	4 tablespoons freshly grated Parmesan cheese
1 tablespoon olive oil	good handful of flat-leafed parsley, roughly chopped, to garnish
1 medium onion, finely chopped	
200 g (7 oz) chestnut mushrooms, halved	

Soak the dried *porcini* mushrooms in the water for 20–30 minutes, then drain the soaking water into a saucepan with the vegetable stock. Heat until simmering.

Heat the butter and oil in a large, good-quality, non-stick frying pan, add the onion and stir-fry over a medium heat for about 15 minutes or until soft. Add all the mushrooms and stir for 1 minute. Add the rice and stir in well, then ladle in a quarter of the stock. Bring to a simmer, and cook, stirring gently, until all the stock is absorbed. Add a little more stock and cook, stirring, until it is absorbed. Continue in this way until all the stock is used up and the rice is tender, moist and creamy. If it isn't tender, add more stock and continue cooking for a few more minutes. Season with salt and pepper, and stir in half the Parmesan cheese, then serve sprinkled with the remaining cheese and garnished with parsley.

NOTES AND TIPS

✦ *Use what mushrooms you can find in this dish; most go very well, although don't use dried Chinese mushrooms.*

✦ *Any good risotto rice will do; Arborio is good-quality and relatively inexpensive.*

NUTRITION

CALORIES PER PORTION: 415	PROTEIN: ★★ FIBRE: ★★ CARBOHYDRATE: ★★★
TOTAL FAT PER PORTION: 15 g	VITAMINS: C, E, A
SATURATED FAT PER PORTION: 5.5 g	MINERALS: K, Zn

Best-ever Vegetable Lasagne

SERVES 4–6

HERE'S how to cook a creamy lasagne with less than one teaspoonful of saturated fat per portion – and it is seriously tasty! Four people would have to be very hungry to eat all this, which is why I've also given nutritional counts for the lasagne to serve six.

1 tablespoon olive oil	1 teaspoon coriander seeds
450 g (1 lb) leeks, sliced	550 ml (1 pint) vegetable stock
2 celery stalks, finely chopped	40 g (1½ oz) low-fat spread
1 clove garlic, peeled and chopped	40 g (1½ oz) plain flour
100 g (3½ oz) brown lentils	700 ml (1¼ pints) skimmed milk
salt and freshly ground black pepper	1 teaspoon mustard powder
400 g (14 oz) can chopped tomatoes	110 g (4 oz) half-fat Cheddar-style cheese, grated
1 tablespoon tomato purée	
225 g (8 oz) small courgettes, sliced	8 sheets 'no-pre-cook' dried lasagne verde
100 g (3½ oz) open-cup mushrooms (see note), sliced	2 tablespoons freshly grated Parmesan cheese

Heat the oil in a large non-stick frying pan, add the leeks, celery and garlic, and stir-fry until soft. Add the lentils and stir, then season with salt and pepper, and add the tomatoes, tomato purée, courgettes and mushrooms. Bring to a simmer. Crush the coriander seeds with a pestle and mortar, and add to the pan with the stock. Stir, cover and simmer for 30 minutes or until the lentils are tender (depending on their age, this could take up to 1 hour).

Meanwhile, to make the cheese sauce, melt the low-fat spread in a saucepan and add the flour, stirring for 1 minute. Add the milk slowly, stirring all the time, until you have a smooth sauce. Add the mustard and Cheddar-style cheese, season with salt and pepper, stir and set aside. The sauce should be quite runny.

When the vegetable mixture is ready, spoon half of it evenly into the base of an oblong lasagne dish, then cover with a layer of lasagne sheets. Spoon the remainder of the vegetable mixture on top, cover with another layer of lasagne sheets, and finally pour the cheese sauce over evenly. Sprinkle the Parmesan over and bake at 190°C/375°F/Gas Mark 5 for 30–40 minutes or until the top is golden and bubbling.

NUTRITION

CALORIES PER PORTION: 550 (4 servings); 360 (6 servings)
TOTAL FAT PER PORTION: 15 g (4 servings); 10 g (6 servings)
SATURATED FAT PER PORTION: 5 g (4 servings); 3.5 g (6 servings)
PROTEIN: ★★★ FIBRE: ★★★ CARBOHYDRATE: ★★★
VITAMINS: B group, C, beta-carotene, E, A
MINERALS: Ca, K, Fe, Mg, Zn

OPPOSITE Mixed Paella (page 115)

Cheese, Potato and Pepper Pie

SERVES 4

ACCOMPANIED with a green salad or fresh green vegetables and bread, this makes an easy and delicious vegetarian meal for a winter family supper.

1 tablespoon olive oil	salt and freshly ground black pepper
2 red onions, thinly sliced	800 g (1¾ lb) potatoes
2 red and 2 yellow peppers, deseeded and sliced	1 tablespoon freshly grated Parmesan cheese
1 clove garlic, peeled and chopped	**For the cheese sauce**
half 400 g (14 oz) can red kidney beans, drained and rinsed, or 125 g (4½ oz) cooked red kidney beans	25 g (1 oz) low-fat spread
	25 g (1 oz) plain flour
400 g (14 oz) can chopped tomatoes with herbs	400 ml (14 fl oz) skimmed milk
	75 g (3 oz) half-fat Cheddar-style cheese, grated
1 tablespoon tomato purée	pinch of mustard powder
dash of soy sauce	salt and freshly ground black pepper
1 teaspoon mustard powder	

Heat the oil in a non-stick frying pan, add the onions, peppers and garlic, and stir-fry until soft. Add the beans, tomatoes, tomato purée, soy sauce and mustard powder. Season with salt and pepper, stir, cover and simmer for 30 minutes, adding a little water if the mixture looks too dry. While the vegetables are simmering, peel the potatoes, cut them into large chunks and cook in lightly salted boiling water until just tender.

While the potatoes and vegetables are cooking, make the cheese sauce. Melt the low-fat spread in a small saucepan, add the flour and cook for 1 minute, stirring. Slowly add the milk, stirring all the time, until you have a smooth sauce. Add the cheese and mustard, and season with salt and pepper. Stir to melt the cheese, then set aside but keep warm.

When the potatoes are just tender, drain them and slice into 1 cm (½ inch) thick rounds. By now the vegetable mixture should be ready, so spoon it into a large soufflé dish (or similar), and top with the sliced potatoes. Pour the cheese sauce over and sprinkle with the Parmesan. Place under a hot grill until the top is bubbling and golden, then serve immediately.

NUTRITION

CALORIES PER PORTION: 440	PROTEIN: ★★★ FIBRE: ★★★ CARBOHYDRATE: ★★★
TOTAL FAT PER PORTION: 10 g	VITAMINS: C, beta-carotene, E, B group
SATURATED FAT PER PORTION: 3 g	MINERALS: Ca, K, Fe, Mg

OPPOSITE Spaghetti with Bacon and Pesto (page 113)

Ratatouille and Lentil Gratin

SERVES 4

THIS is a clever main meal for slimmers, as there is so much to eat you won't believe you're watching your weight. And it is *packed* full of vitamins and minerals.

1 large aubergine	4 tomatoes, skinned (see page 33) and chopped
4 medium courgettes	
salt and freshly ground black pepper	2–3 teaspoons chopped fresh oregano, or 1 teaspoon dried oregano
140 g (5 oz) brown lentils	
1 tablespoon olive oil	125 ml (4½ fl oz) passata
1 large onion, roughly chopped	4 heaped tablespoons dry breadcrumbs
1 green and 1 red pepper, deseeded and sliced	4 tablespoons grated half-fat Cheddar-style cheese
1 clove garlic, peeled and chopped	

Chop the aubergine and courgettes, and place in a colander. Sprinkle with salt, place a weighted plate on top, and leave to drain for at least 30 minutes.

Meanwhile, simmer the lentils in unsalted water for 30 minutes or until tender. Drain the lentils and rinse and dry the aubergine and courgettes.

Heat the oil in a large, non-stick frying pan, add the onion, peppers and garlic, and stir-fry until soft. Add the tomatoes, aubergine, courgettes, oregano and passata, season with salt and pepper, cover and simmer for 30 minutes. Check the seasoning, then spoon half the mixture into a large gratin dish. Arrange the lentils on top, then cover with the rest of the ratatouille. Mix the breadcrumbs with the cheese and sprinkle over the ratatouille. Grill for a few minutes or until the top is golden, then serve.

NOTES AND TIPS

✦ *You could bake the gratin in the oven at 190°C/375°F/Gas Mark 5 for 30 minutes, if you prefer.*

✦ *Serve with salad and crusty French or wholemeal bread.*

NUTRITION

CALORIES PER PORTION: 255	PROTEIN: ★★★ FIBRE: ★★★ CARBOHYDRATE: ★★★
TOTAL FAT PER PORTION: 7.5 g	VITAMINS: beta-carotene, C, E, B group
SATURATED FAT PER PORTION: 2 g	MINERALS: K, Fe, Mg, Zn, Ca

Vegetable Korma

SERVES 4

HERE'S a mild and creamy curry that everyone will enjoy, despite the fact that it is *very* nutritious!

2 aubergines	½ teaspoon chilli powder
salt and freshly ground black pepper	1 knob of fresh root ginger, peeled and finely chopped
1½ tablespoons groundnut oil	
2 medium onions, thinly sliced	300 g (11 oz) potato, peeled, cut into chunks and parboiled
2 cloves garlic, peeled and crushed, then chopped	
1 teaspoon ground cumin	100 g (3½ oz) green beans, cut into 2.5 cm (1 inch) pieces
2 teaspoons ground coriander	400 ml (14 fl oz) vegetable stock
1 teaspoon ground turmeric	25 g (1 oz) blanched almonds
1 teaspoon garam masala	300 g (11 oz) low-fat Greek yogurt

Cut the aubergines into chunks and place in a colander, sprinkling with salt. Place a weighted plate on top and leave to drain for at least 30 minutes. Rinse and dry with kitchen paper.

Heat the oil in a large, non-stick, lidded sauté pan, add the onions and garlic, and stir-fry until soft. Add all the dry spices and the ginger, and stir-fry for 1–2 minutes. Add the aubergines, potato chunks and green beans, and pour over half the stock. Stir, cover and simmer for 15 minutes. Slice the almonds in half and add to the pan. Cover and cook for a further 15 minutes, adding more stock as necessary to make a nice rich sauce.

Before serving, stir in the yogurt and heat through gently.

NOTES AND TIPS

✦ *It's best if you can grind your own spices, but, if not, buy ready-ground spices regularly. If you keep them too long (especially in light, hot conditions), they lose their aroma and flavour.*

✦ *Serve with basmati rice and/or chapatis warmed in the oven or microwave.*

NUTRITION

CALORIES PER PORTION: **280**	PROTEIN: ★ FIBRE: ★★★ CARBOHYDRATE: ★★
TOTAL FAT PER PORTION: **13.5 g**	VITAMINS: C, beta-carotene, E
SATURATED FAT PER PORTION: **3.5 g**	MINERALS: K, Zn, Mg, Ca, Fe

Mixed Vegetables with a Spicy Stuffing

SERVES 4

THIS vegan recipe is so saintly – no dairy produce, no cholesterol, hardly any saturated fats – that I thought twice about including it in this book, bearing in mind my moderate approach. However, it *is* good enough to eat, and will bring you back for seconds. So it gets in!

4 large open-cap mushrooms	450 ml (16 fl oz) vegetable stock
1½ tablespoons olive oil	50 g (2 oz) sultanas
4 small yellow peppers	½ teaspoon ground cinnamon
4 medium courgettes	1 teaspoon ground cumin
1 medium onion, chopped	1 teaspoon Chinese five-spice powder
1 large clove garlic, peeled and crushed	1 tablespoon chopped fresh parsley
225 g (8 oz) Arborio rice	1 tablespoon chopped fresh mint
1 beef tomato, skinned (see page 33) and chopped	pinch of sugar
	salt and freshly ground black pepper
25 g (1 oz) pine nuts	fresh parsley, to garnish
2 teaspoons tomato purée	

First, prepare the vegetables for stuffing. Remove the stems from the mushrooms, and wipe the caps dry. Brush the outsides and rims of the mushroom caps with a little of the olive oil and place in a small baking dish. Cut the tops off the peppers and remove the seeds. Cut the stalks off so that the peppers will stand firmly. Cut the top third off each courgette (lengthways), scoop out half of the flesh and discard.

To make the stuffing, heat the remaining oil in a large, non-stick frying pan, add the onion and garlic, and stir-fry until soft and just turning golden. Add the rice and stir, then add the tomato, pine nuts, tomato purée, stock, sultanas, spices, herbs and sugar. Season with salt and pepper, and simmer, uncovered, for 30 minutes, stirring occasionally and adding extra stock or water if needed. Meanwhile, preheat the oven to 190°C/375°F/ Gas Mark 5. Check the seasoning of the stuffing, then spoon the mixture carefully into the mushrooms, peppers and courgettes.

Place the peppers in a baking dish, add a little water or stock to surround them, cover and cook in the oven for 20 minutes. Remove the baking dish from the oven, and add the stuffed courgettes to the same dish as the peppers. Cover and return to the oven for a further 15 minutes. Put the mushrooms, covered, in the oven, too, and bake for a final 15 minutes or until all the vegetables are tender. Serve one mushroom, one pepper and one courgette to each person, garnished with parsley.

NOTES AND TIPS

✦ *To cut down the cooking time for the peppers, you could blanch them in boiling water for 3 minutes, then fill them and put them in the oven at the same time as the courgettes.*

✦ *Serve with crusty bread and salad.*

✦ *You can use red instead of yellow peppers, and small squash instead of the courgettes.*

NUTRITION

CALORIES PER PORTION: 410	PROTEIN: ★ FIBRE: ★★ CARBOHYDRATE: ★★★
TOTAL FAT PER PORTION: 12 g	VITAMINS: beta-carotene, C, E, B group
SATURATED FAT PER PORTION: 1.5 g	MINERALS: K, Fe, Mg, Zn

Colcannon

SERVES 4

HERE'S an iron-rich Irish recipe that's a bit like bubble and squeak. I've added protein with some cheese and an egg, to make what would be a snack into a real supper. It's so easy to do — why not get the children to make it for you?

650 g (1½ lb) old potatoes	15 g (½ oz) low-salt butter
4 shallots, peeled and very finely chopped	60 g (2½ oz) half-fat Cheddar-style cheese, grated
100 ml (3½ fl oz) skimmed milk	450 g (1 lb) tender spring greens, finely shredded
1 size-3 egg, beaten	
pinch of freshly grated nutmeg	
salt and freshly ground black pepper	

Preheat the oven to 200°C/400°F/Gas Mark 6. Meanwhile peel the potatoes, cut them into chunks and boil them in lightly salted water until tender. Drain and mash with the shallots, milk, egg, nutmeg, salt and pepper, butter and half the cheese. Cook the greens in a very little boiling water for 3 minutes, then drain and mix into the potatoes. Pile the mixture into a baking dish, sprinkle on the remaining cheese and bake in the oven at 200°C/400°F/Gas Mark 6 for 20 minutes or until the top is golden.

NOTES AND TIPS

✦ *You could use sprouts or savoy cabbage instead of the greens.*

NUTRITION

CALORIES PER PORTION: 285	PROTEIN: ★★★ FIBRE: ★★★ CARBOHYDRATE: ★★★
TOTAL FAT PER PORTION: 8 g	VITAMINS: C, beta-carotene, folic acid
SATURATED FAT PER PORTION: 4 g	MINERALS: Fe, Ca, K

Oriental Stir-fry

SERVES 4

YOU may wonder why this recipe is relatively high in fat when it is full of so many low-fat vegetables and carbohydrates. Well, it's the almonds and seeds – both high in fat, but mostly the very-good-for-you, mono-unsaturated kind. Nuts and seeds are also one of our best sources of vitamin E. So eat and enjoy.

175 g (6 oz) medium egg thread noodles	50 g (2 oz) water chestnuts, halved, or bamboo shoots
1½ tablespoons sesame oil	1 tablespoon lemon juice
1 red pepper, deseeded and sliced	2 tablespoons light soy sauce
75 g (3 oz) green beans or mangetout	125 g (4½ oz) blanched almonds
200 g (7 oz) broccoli florets or courgettes	1 teaspoon runny honey
1 large leek, sliced	1 tablespoon toasted sesame seeds
100 g (3½ oz) mushrooms, sliced	
1 clove garlic, peeled and crushed	
small knob of fresh root ginger, peeled and chopped	

Put the noodles on to soak or boil according to packet instructions, drain when ready and keep warm.

Heat the oil in a wok or large, non-stick frying pan, add the red pepper, beans (or mangetout), broccoli (or courgettes) and leek, and stir-fry for 2 minutes. Add the mushrooms, garlic, ginger, chestnuts, lemon juice and soy sauce, and stir-fry for a further 2 minutes. Add the blanched almonds and honey, and stir again for 1 minute. Stir in the sesame seeds and serve the stir-fry on the noodles.

NOTES AND TIPS

✦ *If you like a less dry stir-fry, you can add a little vegetable stock blended with 1 teaspoon cornflour after you've added the honey.*

✦ *Water chestnuts are not nuts as such, and are low in fat and calories.*

✦ *Rice noodles make a nice change from egg noodles – most supermarkets and delicatessens sell them.*

NUTRITION

CALORIES PER PORTION: 475	PROTEIN: ★★ FIBRE: ★★★ CARBOHYDRATE: ★★★
TOTAL FAT PER PORTION: 27 g	VITAMINS: B group, E, C, beta-carotene
SATURATED FAT PER PORTION: 3.5 g	MINERALS: Zn, Ca, K, Mg, Fe

Pumpkin, Spinach and Cauliflower Bake

SERVES 4

I GREW pumpkins for the first time this year and now I'm hooked – baked, boiled, mashed, or whatever, they taste superb and are full of beta-carotene and other 'good-for-yous'. Don't be tempted to use chopped spinach in this recipe – it won't work.

500 g (18 oz) peeled pumpkin, cubed	**For the white sauce**
salt and freshly ground black pepper	700 ml (1¼ pints) skimmed milk
25 g (1 oz) low-fat spread	1 small onion, peeled
1 cauliflower, cut into florets	1 teaspoon mustard powder
400 g (14 oz) leaf spinach, fresh or frozen	salt and freshly ground black pepper
4 tablespoons dry wholemeal breadcrumbs	40 g (1½ oz) low-fat spread
2 tablespoons chopped hazelnuts or mixed nuts	40 g (1½ oz) plain flour

Preheat the oven to 190°C/375°F/Gas Mark 5. Meanwhile prepare the vegetables. Cook the pumpkin pieces in boiling water until tender, then drain, season with salt and pepper, and mash with the low-fat spread. Cook the cauliflower in lightly salted boiling water for about 3 minutes or until barely cooked. Drain. Put fresh spinach in a pan with a drop of water, cover and heat until just wilted. Drain. Heat frozen spinach until thawed.

To make the white sauce, put the milk in a saucepan with the onion and mustard. Season with salt and pepper, and bring almost to the boil, then remove from the heat and leave to infuse. Melt the low-fat spread in a small saucepan, add the flour and cook, stirring, for 1–2 minutes. Gradually strain in the milk, stirring all the time until you have a smooth sauce. Check the seasoning.

Arrange half the spinach in the bottom of a suitably sized baking dish. Cover with all the pumpkin, then all the cauliflower. Stir the rest of the spinach into the white sauce, and pour over the dish, smoothing evenly. Top with the breadcrumbs and nuts, and bake in the oven for 20 minutes or until the topping is lightly browned and the sauce is bubbling. Serve at once.

NUTRITION

CALORIES PER PORTION: 265	PROTEIN: ★★★ FIBRE: ★★ CARBOHYDRATE: ★★
TOTAL FAT PER PORTION: 11.5 g	VITAMINS: beta-carotene, B group, C, E
SATURATED FAT PER PORTION: 2.5 g	MINERALS: K, Ca, Fe, Zn, Mg

CHAPTER 8

PASTA, RICE AND GRAINS

P asta, rice and other grains, such as couscous, are not only delicious and quick and relatively easy to cook, but they also happen to be *good, healthy* food. The whole grain varieties are natural foods, high in complex carbohydrates and low in fat and calories – and even the 'white' versions of pasta and rice are good, too.

Pasta, both white and whole wheat, has the benefit of being a food that takes time to be absorbed by your digestive system, so it is invaluable for slimmers and for people who tend to get hungry between meals. A pasta dish a day keeps the hunger pangs at bay! Pasta and grains are not high in calories, either, so don't let anyone tell you they are 'fattening'! True, many of the traditional sauces for pasta, and traditional rice dishes, are high in fat, but here's where we discover how to turn those traditional dishes, like lasagne and paella, into healthy, low-fat dishes, and I've come up with plenty of *new* ideas.

Pasta Notes

When buying pasta, buy the best quality you can get. Dried pasta is fine, but read the label and make sure you are buying '100 per cent durum wheat' pasta. This gives by far the best texture and flavour when cooked.

Depending on which type and size of dried pasta you buy, it cooks in 8–15 minutes. Read the packet instructions carefully and be sure to use *plenty* of lightly salted boiling water. Stir it well after it has been put in the pan, or the pieces will tend to stick together, then leave the lid off and keep the water boiling fast.

Bought fresh pasta can be good, or it can be worse than any cheap dried variety, so if you like fresh pasta, shop around.

Rice Notes

Different rices suit different occasions, and, as they store well, you can keep a variety of rices in the cupboard to suit whatever you choose to cook. My short list of essentials would have to be: basmati, long-grain and wild rice mixed; risotto rice, e.g. Arborio; plain long-grain rice; brown rice; Thai fragrant rice.

Noodles and Other Grains

Don't forget to keep a stock of dried egg and rice noodles in the storecupboard, too, for Chinese-style meals and soups. If you're busy, noodles are even quicker to cook than pasta and you can use them in similar ways – or use them instead of rice in the ideas above. And it's worth keeping grains other than rice, too – such as couscous, buckwheat, millet and bulghar. They all make an alternative to rice and offer a variety of different nutrients.

Nutrition Notes

All pasta and grains are excellent sources of carbohydrate and reasonable sources of protein. White pastas and grains have less vitamins and minerals in them than their whole grain counterparts.

White pasta per 100 g (3½ oz), raw weight: Carbohydrate 74 g; Protein 12 g; Fibre 2.9 g; Vitamins B_1, B_3 and folic acid; Minerals K, Mg, Ca, Fe, Zn.

Whole wheat pasta per 100 g (3½ oz), raw: Carbohydrate 66 g; Protein 13.5 g; Fibre 8.4 g; Vitamins as white pasta but more of them; Minerals as white pasta but more of them.

White rice per 100 g (3½ oz), raw: Carbohydrate 87 g; Protein 6.5 g; Fibre 0.5 g; Vitamin B_3; Minerals K, Zn.

Brown rice per 100 g (3½ oz) raw: Carbohydrate 81 g; Protein 6.7 g; Fibre 1.9 g; Vitamins B_1, B_3, folic acid, E; Minerals K, Mg, Fe, Zn.

CALORIE AND FAT COUNTS FOR PASTA, RICE AND GRAINS

Raw weight pasta and grains, per 25 g (1 oz)

	Cals	Fat (grams)
Rice, white	90	0.7
Rice, brown	89	0.7
Pasta, white or verde	85	0.5
Pasta, whole wheat	81	0.6
Egg noodles	97	2.0
Couscous	94	0.5

table continues

Accompaniments

	Cals	Fat (grams)
Tomato Sauce (page 110), 1 serving	51	trace
Olive oil, 1 tablespoon	135	15.0
Olives, per olive	3	0.3
Parmesan cheese, grated, 1 tablespoon	30	2.2
Pecorino cheese, grated, 1 tablespoon	30	2.2
Pesto, ready-made, 1 tablespoon	70	6.5
Pine nuts, 1 tablespoon (6 g/¼ oz)	42	4.2
Sun-dried tomatoes, drained, each	15	1.5

Restaurant meals (all counts approximate)

Cannelloni with meat and cheese sauce	600	high
Pasta carbonara	800–1000	high
Lasagne	800	high
Napoletana	600	medium
Spaghetti bolognese	800	high
Marinara	600	medium
Chicken risotto	700	medium/high
Mushroom risotto	600	medium
Paella	800	medium
Special fried rice, side dish	500	high
Special fried noodles, side dish	500	high

Pasta Harlequin Bake

SERVES 4

HERE is a glorified version of macaroni cheese that contains less fat and more fibre and vitamins than the original. It makes a quick family supper, ideal for budding cooks to try making themselves.

225 g (8 oz) macaroni	40 g (1½ oz) plain flour
salt	700 ml (1¼ pints) skimmed milk
225 g (8 oz) broccoli florets	1 teaspoon mustard powder
1 large red and 1 large yellow pepper, deseeded and cut into 2.5 cm (1 inch) slices	110 g (4 oz) half-fat Cheddar-style cheese, grated
25 g (1 oz) fresh wholemeal breadcrumbs	salt and freshly ground black pepper
1 tablespoon freshly grated Parmesan cheese	
For the cheese sauce	
40 g (1½ oz) low-fat spread	

Preheat the oven to 190°C/375°F/Gas Mark 5.

Cook the macaroni in plenty of lightly salted boiling water for about 10 minutes or until *al dente*. Drain and arrange in a large gratin or lasagne dish. Parboil the broccoli and peppers for 3 minutes, then drain and arrange with the pasta.

To make the cheese sauce, melt the low-fat spread in a saucepan, add the flour and cook, stirring, for 1–2 minutes. Gradually add the milk, stirring all the time, until you have a smooth sauce. Add the mustard and Cheddar-style cheese, season with salt and pepper, and stir. Pour the sauce evenly over the macaroni and vegetables, and then sprinkle on the breadcrumbs and Parmesan cheese. Bake in the oven for 30 minutes or until the top is golden and the sauce is bubbling.

NOTES AND TIPS

✦ *When you first add some milk to the fat and flour roux, the sauce may seem impossibly lumpy, but I promise if you keep adding the milk gradually, stirring all the time with a good wooden spoon, it will soon turn into a smooth sauce. It also helps if the milk is warmed before making the sauce. The finished sauce will be quite runny, but don't worry, it is supposed to be.*

NUTRITION

CALORIES PER PORTION: 455
TOTAL FAT PER PORTION: 11 g
SATURATED FAT PER PORTION: 4.5 g

PROTEIN: ★★★ FIBRE: ★★ CARBOHYDRATE: ★★★
VITAMINS: B group, beta-carotene, C, E
MINERALS: K, Ca, Fe, Zn, Mg

Baked Pasta with Smoked Haddock and Peas

SERVES 4

THIS makes an easy change from haddock, chips and peas. It's lower in fat and higher in calcium, but if you're salt-watching, make sure you choose low-salt dishes for the rest of the day.

225 g (8 oz) dried penne (pasta 'quills')	about 700 ml (1¼ pints) skimmed milk
salt and freshly ground black pepper	1 teaspoon mustard powder
100 g (3½ oz) frozen peas	450 g (1 lb) smoked haddock fillet
40 g (1½ oz) low-fat spread	2 tablespoons freshly grated Parmesan cheese
40 g (1½ oz) plain flour	a little seasoning, to taste

Preheat the oven to 190°C/375°F/Gas Mark 5.

Cook the pasta in plenty of lightly salted boiling water for about 12 minutes or until just tender. Drain. Cook the peas in boiling water until tender, then drain.

Melt the low-fat spread in a saucepan and add the flour. Cook, stirring, for 1–2 minutes, then gradually add the milk, stirring all the time, until you have a smooth sauce. Add the mustard, season with salt and pepper, and if you have anything other than a quite runny sauce, thin it down a little with some extra skimmed milk.

Cut the fish into bite-sized chunks and arrange with the pasta and peas in a shallow, ovenproof dish. Cover with the sauce, and sprinkle the cheese on top. Bake in the oven for 20–30 minutes or until the top is golden and bubbling.

NOTES AND TIPS

✦ *If you like, you could use salmon, tuna or even an unsmoked white fish in this dish.*
✦ *Go easy on the salt in this dish as smoked haddock is quite salty.*
✦ *Serve with a green salad.*

NUTRITION

CALORIES PER PORTION: 475   PROTEIN: ★★★ FIBRE: ★★ CARBOHYDRATE: ★★★
TOTAL FAT PER PORTION: 7.7 g   VITAMINS: B group, C, beta-carotene
SATURATED FAT PER PORTION: 2.5 g   MINERALS: Zn, Ca, K, Fe, Mg

Note: This recipes contains approximately 1850 mg sodium per portion.

Jumbo Pasta Shells with Tuna and Olives

SERVES 4

THIS is an unusual way to serve tuna and pasta. You can now buy tuna canned in water rather than brine, which is useful if you are watching your salt intake. This is a good slimmer's dish as it is low in fat and calories, but there is plenty to eat.

½ quantity Tomato Sauce (see page 110)	150 g (5½ oz) tub Shape low-fat soft cheese
300 g (11 oz) can tuna in water or brine, drained	2 tablespoons 8 per cent fat fromage frais
handful of fresh flat-leafed parsley, chopped	mixed salad leaves, to serve
20 dried jumbo pasta shells (about 110 g/4 oz)	10 black olives, halved and stoned
salt	

Make the tomato sauce (see page 110), but don't put it through the blender. Mix it in a bowl with the tuna and parsley, and keep warm. Cook the pasta shells in plenty of boiling salted water for about 15 minutes or until tender. Drain.

Melt the Shape cheese and fromage frais together in a saucepan. Meanwhile, arrange the salad leaves on serving plates, fill each of the pasta shells with some of the tuna mixture, and set five shells on each plate. Pour a trickle of the cheese sauce over each shell and top each with an olive half. Serve warm.

NOTES AND TIPS

✦ *If you can't get hold of any jumbo pasta shells, use small shells and, instead of filling them, simply toss them with the tomato sauce and pour the cheese over to serve, topped with the olives.*

✦ *Some crusty* ciabatta *makes the perfect accompaniment, and increases the carbohydrate total.*

✦ *Melted Shape makes a good cheese sauce for all kinds of occasions. However, I find it a little salty, so I mix it with fromage frais, making it go further as well. You needn't feel guilty about using convenience foods occasionally!*

NUTRITION

CALORIES PER PORTION: 260	PROTEIN: ★★★ FIBRE: ★★ CARBOHYDRATE: ★★
TOTAL FAT PER PORTION: 4 g	VITAMINS: B group, beta-carotene, C, E, D
SATURATED FAT PER PORTION: 2 g	MINERALS: K, Ca, Mg, Fe

Fusilli Napoletana

SERVES 4

PASTA with a simple tomato sauce is still one of my very favourite quick dishes. The tomato sauce I've used here gives a creamy finish without using extra fat, thus allowing you to add some shaved Italian cheese to your serving!

300 g (11 oz) dried fusilli (pasta 'spirals')	1 large onion, finely chopped
salt	1 large clove garlic, peeled and finely chopped
4 tablespoons freshly grated Parmesan or Pecorino cheese	1 small celery stalk, finely chopped
roughly chopped fresh basil or parsley, to garnish	1 tablespoon tomato purée
	1 teaspoon brown sugar
For the tomato sauce	salt and freshly ground black pepper
550 g (1¼ lb) can best-quality chopped Italian tomatoes	1 teaspoon dried basil or a few sprigs fresh basil, chopped

Put all the sauce ingredients in a saucepan, and simmer gently for at least 30 minutes (longer if you can, up to 1 hour), stirring from time to time. Cool slightly, then purée in a blender. Return to the pan to reheat.

Cook the pasta in plenty of lightly salted boiling water for about 10 minutes or until *al dente*. Drain and serve, topped with the reheated sauce, cheese and garnish.

NOTES AND TIPS
+ *You can thin the sauce down a little with passata if you like.*
+ *Garlic fans can increase the garlic.*
+ *The tomato sauce can be frozen so it's worth making a large batch.*

NUTRITION

CALORIES PER PORTION: 337	PROTEIN: ★★★ FIBRE: ★★ CARBOHYDRATE: ★★★
TOTAL FAT PER PORTION: 4 g	VITAMINS: B group, beta-carotene, C, E
SATURATED FAT PER PORTION: 1.5 g	MINERALS: K, Ca, Mg, Fe

Classic Lasagne

SERVES 4–6

LASAGNE is normally extremely high in both calories and fat. This version is still moderately high in fat, but if eaten on a day when lunch is 'light and low' it won't send your fat-count sky-high. On the plus side, it's packed full of goodies.

1 quantity Cheese Sauce (see page 107)	100 g (3½ oz) mushrooms, sliced
1 quantity Tomato Sauce (see page 110)	275 ml (½ pint) beef stock
1 tablespoon olive oil	8 sheets no-pre-cook lasagne
325 g (12 oz) extra-lean minced beef	1 tablespoon freshly grated Parmesan cheese
100 g (3½ oz) carrot, finely chopped	

Make the cheese sauce as on page 107. Make the tomato sauce as on page 110, but don't put it through the blender.

Heat the oil in a non-stick frying pan, add the beef, and fry until browned, stirring to break up the meat. Add the carrot and mushrooms, and stir again, then add the tomato sauce and stock. Simmer for at least 30 minutes or until you have a not-too-thick, meaty sauce. Check the seasoning.

Preheat the oven to 190°C/375°F/Gas Mark 5. Spoon half the beef sauce evenly in the bottom of a lasagne dish and cover with half the lasagne. Top with the remaining meat sauce, and cover again with the remaining lasagne. Pour the cheese sauce over and sprinkle on the Parmesan. Bake in the oven for 30 minutes or until the top is golden and bubbling.

NOTES AND TIPS

✦ *You can also use this beef sauce to fill jumbo pasta shells (see page 109) or as a bolognese sauce.*

NUTRITION

CALORIES PER PORTION: 560 (4 servings); 370 (6 servings)
TOTAL FAT PER PORTION: 17.5 g (4 servings); 12 g (6 servings)
SATURATED FAT PER PORTION: 7 g (4 servings); 4.5 g (6 servings)

PROTEIN: ★★★ FIBRE: ★★
CARBOHYDRATE: ★★
VITAMINS: B group, beta-carotene, C, E
MINERALS: K, Fe, Ca, Mg

Creamy Tagliatelle with Scallops and Spinach

SERVES 4

TRADITIONAL pasta cream sauces use loads of double cream and butter, and sometimes eggs. This one has a delicate creamy, cheesy flavour that goes well with the sweetness of scallops but isn't fatty at all. If you're not watching your weight, you could divide this recipe between two or three people.

240 g (8½ oz) dried orange and white tagliatelle	3 tablespoons half-fat crème fraîche
salt and freshly ground black pepper	3 tablespoons 8 per cent fat fromage frais
125 g (4½ oz) fresh or frozen leaf spinach	2 tablespoons crumbled dolcelatte cheese
1 tablespoon corn or sunflower oil	100 g (3½ oz) small mushrooms, halved
2 shallots, peeled and very finely chopped	300 g (11 oz) scallops, fresh if possible, halved if large

Cook the tagliatelle in plenty of lightly salted boiling water for about 8 minutes or until *al dente*. Put the spinach in a saucepan with a very little water, cover and heat until just wilted. Heat frozen spinach until thawed. Drain, add to the pasta and combine.

Heat the oil in a non-stick frying pan, add the shallots and stir-fry for 2 minutes. Remove from the heat. Put the crème fraîche, fromage frais, cheese and mushrooms in a small saucepan. Season with salt and pepper, and heat until you have a creamy sauce. Keep warm. Return the frying pan containing the shallots to the heat, add the scallops, and stir-fry for 2–3 minutes or until the scallops are just cooked through.

Turn the pasta into a serving bowl, spoon the scallops and onion on top, then top with the sauce. Stir through to combine lightly before serving.

NOTES AND TIPS

✦ *Scallops are a bit of a luxury, but a little goes a long way. Fresh are by far the best; buy the biggest ones you can – tiny little frozen ones may shrink and be a disaster.*

✦ *Whatever you do, don't overcook scallops. They can take a high heat, but only for a short while. Long cooking – whether over a high or low heat – will make them tough.*

✦ *Cooked chicken meat could be used instead of the scallops.*

NUTRITION

CALORIES PER PORTION: 365	PROTEIN: ★★★ FIBRE: ★★ CARBOHYDRATE: ★★★
TOTAL FAT PER PORTION: 11 g	VITAMINS: B$_1$, folic acid, C
SATURATED FAT PER PORTION: 4.5 g	MINERALS: K, Ca, Mg, Zn, Fe

Spaghetti with Bacon and Pesto

SERVES 4

HOW can a dish be healthy when it contains bacon, hard cheese and oil? Easy! It's all about buying wisely and getting your proportions right. This dish is healthy because it's full of complex carbohydrates, vitamins, minerals, fibre and mono-unsaturated oil. *Don't* always avoid oil – it's *good for you!*

300 g (11 oz) dried short spaghetti	**For the pesto**
salt	4 cloves garlic, peeled
100 g (3½ oz) broccoli, broken into small florets	about 25 g (1 oz) fresh basil (1 pack), roughly chopped
50 g (2 oz) frozen petits pois	
1 teaspoon corn oil	75 g (3 oz) Parmesan cheese, grated
150 g (5½ oz) low-salt, extra-lean back bacon, derinded and cut into strips	4 medium tomatoes, skinned (see page 33), deseeded and chopped
8 cherry tomatoes, halved	40 ml (1½ fl oz) olive oil
fresh basil leaves, to garnish	

To make the pesto, pound all the ingredients together with a pestle and mortar until you have a thick paste.

Cook the spaghetti in a large saucepan of lightly salted boiling water for 8–10 minutes or until just cooked. Meanwhile, put the broccoli and peas in a very little water and steam for 2–3 minutes. Drain and keep warm. Brush the base of a non-stick frying pan with the corn oil and add the bacon strips. Slowly heat the pan until the bacon begins to cook, turning up the heat as it does so. Stir once or twice until the bacon is crisp.

Drain the pasta and tip into a serving bowl. Pour over the pesto and add the bacon and all the vegetables. Garnish with basil leaves and serve immediately.

NOTES AND TIPS
✦ *You can try different pastas with this sauce, e.g. tagliatelle or macaroni. The spinach pasta (verde) varieties are also very good.*

--- **NUTRITION** ---

CALORIES PER PORTION: 520	PROTEIN: ★★★ FIBRE: ★★ CARBOHYDRATE: ★★★
TOTAL FAT PER PORTION: 21 g	VITAMINS: B$_3$, folic acid, beta-carotene, C, E
SATURATED FAT PER PORTION: 6.5 g	MINERALS: K, Fe, Zn, Ca, Mg

Seafood Risotto

SERVES 4

IT'S NICE that something as delicious as this is relatively low in fat – 27 per cent. It's also stuffed with minerals. However, it is quite low in fibre (that's because risotto rice doesn't contain a lot of fibre), so make sure you have a salad with it and that the rest of your day's meals are high fibre (see list on page 11).

15 g (½ oz) butter	100 g (3½ oz) dressed crabmeat (brown and white)
1 tablespoon olive oil	
1 litre (1¾ pints) fish stock	225 g (8 oz) cooked peeled prawns
2 shallots, peeled and finely chopped	100 g (3½ oz) shelled mussels
1 celery stalk, finely chopped	4 tablespoons half-fat crème fraîche
300 g (11 oz) Arborio rice	2 teaspoons lemon juice
salt and freshly ground black pepper	2 tablespoons freshly grated Parmesan cheese

Heat the butter and oil in a large frying pan. Meanwhile, put the stock in a saucepan and bring to a simmer. Add the shallots and celery to the oil, and stir-fry until soft, then add the rice, season with salt and pepper, and stir well. Add a few ladlefuls of the stock, stir and bring to a simmer. Simmer, stirring, until all the stock is absorbed. Add more stock and simmer, stirring, until it is absorbed. Keep the heat as low as possible so that the rice doesn't stick. Continue in this way until all the stock is absorbed and the rice is creamy and tender.

Add all the fish and stir gently for 1 minute to heat through. Add the crème fraîche and lemon juice, and stir again. Serve with the cheese sprinkled over.

NOTES AND TIPS

✦ *If using raw prawns, add them for the last 5 minutes of cooking.*
✦ *You can use squid or cockles instead of the mussels.*

NUTRITION

CALORIES PER PORTION: 490	PROTEIN: ★★★ FIBRE: ★ CARBOHYDRATE: ★★★
TOTAL FAT PER PORTION: 15 g	VITAMINS: B group, C, E
SATURATED FAT PER PORTION: 5.5 g	MINERALS: K, Zn, Ca, Mg, Fe

Note: This dish contains 162 mg cholesterol and 1365 mg sodium per portion.

Mixed Paella

SERVES 4

THERE'S a different version of 'paella' for every day of the year, although the classic Spanish version contains little except rice, pork or chicken, fish and saffron. This one's pretty straightforward, too, and contains less than 20 per cent fat and 5 per cent saturates. If you enjoy paella, it helps if you invest in a real paella pan.

1 sachet saffron strands	about 825 ml (1½ pints) chicken stock
1 tablespoon olive oil	2 medium tomatoes, skinned (see page 33) and chopped
250 g (9 oz) raw chicken or pork meat, no skin or bone	salt and freshly ground black pepper
1 onion, finely chopped	100 g (3½ oz) frozen peas, thawed
2 cloves garlic, peeled and crushed, then chopped	200 g (7 oz) frozen mixed seafood, thawed
1 small red pepper, deseeded and chopped	8 jumbo prawns, tails left on
275 g (10 oz) long-grain rice	

Steep the saffron in a little boiling water. Heat the oil in a paella pan or enormous frying pan (or two frying pans), add the chicken or pork pieces, and fry until golden. Remove the meat from the pan with a slotted spatula.

Add the onion, garlic and red pepper to the pan, and stir-fry for a few minutes. Add the rice, stir again, and return the chicken to the pan with the stock, saffron infusion and tomato. Season with salt and pepper, and simmer for 15 minutes.

Add the peas and mixed seafood and stir, adding extra stock if necessary. (If your large prawns are raw, add them now.) Simmer until the rice is tender and the liquid is virtually all absorbed. Add the prawns (if cooked) to heat through. Serve.

NOTES AND TIPS

✦ *The appearance of this dish is improved if you add some fresh mussels in their shells. Buy about 20, scrub them and remove the beards. Tap them and discard any that don't close. Add the mussels to the pan for the last 2 minutes of cooking time; when the shells open, they are ready. This will add 20 calories per portion and negligible fat.*

NUTRITION

CALORIES PER PORTION: 470	PROTEIN: ★★★ FIBRE: ★★ CARBOHYDRATE: ★★★
TOTAL FAT PER PORTION: 9.5 g	VITAMINS: B group, beta-carotene, C
SATURATED FAT PER PORTION: 2.5 g	MINERALS: Ca, Fe, Zn, K

Chilli Rice and Chickpeas

SERVES 4

I ENJOY chilli beans tremendously. When you mix them with rice you get a 'complete protein', as well as a gorgeous, inexpensive low-fat supper.

1 tablespoon corn oil	100 g (3½ oz) drained canned black-eye beans
1 red onion, chopped	400 g (14 oz) can chickpeas, drained
1 clove garlic, peeled and chopped	110 g (4 oz) basmati rice
1 teaspoon ground allspice	400 g (14 oz) can chopped tomatoes
1 red pepper, deseeded and chopped	salt and freshly ground black pepper
1 or more fresh red chillies, deseeded and chopped	175 ml (6 fl oz) vegetable stock
100 g (3½ oz) frozen sweetcorn kernels	chopped fresh parsley, to garnish

Heat the oil in a lidded, non-stick frying pan or flameproof casserole, add the onion and garlic, and stir-fry for a few minutes or until soft. Add the allspice and stir, then add all the remaining ingredients, except the parsley, cover and simmer for 30 minutes or until the rice is cooked and the dish is still moist. Garnish with lots of parsley.

NOTES AND TIPS

✦ *Black beans or even green lentils would make a nice change from the black-eye beans.*

--- **NUTRITION** ---

CALORIES PER PORTION: 305
TOTAL FAT PER PORTION: 7 g
SATURATED FAT PER PORTION: 1.5 g

PROTEIN: ★★ FIBRE: ★★ CARBOHYDRATE: ★★★
VITAMINS: B₃, folic acid, beta-carotene, C, E
MINERALS: K, Zn, Ca, Fe, Mg

Apricot Pilau

SERVES 4 AS A SIDE DISH

THIS 'pilau' is a heavenly mix of rice, fruit and nuts, high in fibre and iron. It goes well with all kinds of grills and kebabs, and the Aromatic Turkey with Citrus Sauce on page 71.

1 tablespoon groundnut oil	225 g (8 oz) basmati or brown rice
1 onion, finely chopped	500 ml (18 fl oz) vegetable stock
1 clove garlic, peeled and finely chopped	75 g (3 oz) ready-to-eat dried apricots, chopped
½ teaspoon ground cinnamon	25 g (1 oz) pine nuts
½ teaspoon ground cumin	salt and freshly ground black pepper
1 teaspoon ground turmeric	
1 cardamom pod	

Heat the oil in a non-stick frying pan, add the onion, and stir-fry until soft. Add the garlic and spices, and stir for 1 minute. Add the rice and a small amount of the stock, and stir again. Add the apricots and nuts, salt and pepper, and the rest of the stock. Stir, cover and simmer for 20 minutes or until the rice is tender and all the stock is absorbed.

NOTES AND TIPS

✦ *Brown rice contains four times the fibre and more B vitamins than white rice.*
✦ *You can add diced cooked meat or vegetables to this dish to make a quick supper.*

NUTRITION

CALORIES PER PORTION: 330	PROTEIN: ★ FIBRE: ★★ CARBOHYDRATE: ★★★
TOTAL FAT PER PORTION: 10 g	VITAMINS: B$_3$, A, E
SATURATED FAT PER PORTION: 1.5 g	MINERALS: K (Zn if brown rice used)

Spicy Kedgeree

SERVES 4

KEDGEREE was traditionally served as a breakfast dish, but now it makes a perfect lunch or supper. My version is spiced up a bit more than was usual, and I think benefits from it.

1 tablespoon corn oil	125 g (4½ oz) petits pois
1 medium onion, finely chopped	40 g (1½ oz) sultanas
1 clove garlic, peeled and finely chopped	2 size–3 eggs, hard-boiled and roughly chopped
2 teaspoons mild curry powder	
225 g (8 oz) basmati rice	25 g (1 oz) flaked almonds
750 ml (26½ fl oz) light stock	salt and freshly ground black pepper
450 g (1 lb) smoked haddock fillet, diced	chopped fresh parsley, to garnish

Heat the oil in a large, lidded non-stick frying pan, add the onion and garlic, and stir-fry until soft. Add the curry powder and cook, stirring, for 1 minute, then add the rice and stir. Add the stock, cover, and simmer for 20 minutes.

Add the haddock, peas and sultanas, and cook for a further 15 minutes. Finally, add the egg and almonds, and season with salt and pepper. Serve when the rice is completely tender and the fish cooked. Garnish with parsley.

NUTRITION

CALORIES PER PORTION: 485	PROTEIN: ★★★ FIBRE: ★★ CARBOHYDRATE: ★★★
TOTAL FAT PER PORTION: 13 g	VITAMINS: A, B group, D, E
SATURATED FAT PER PORTION: 3 g	MINERALS: Fe, K, Mg, Ca, Zn

Note: This recipe contains 185 mg cholesterol and 1690 mg sodium per portion.

Couscous with Chicken and Vegetables

SERVES 4

COUSCOUS can be quite bland, but if you soak it in stock it can be delicate and delicious. This is a slightly short-cut version of the traditional Moroccan dish – a complete meal which needs nothing with it other than a glass of wine!

1½ tablespoons olive oil	2 tablespoons raisins
4 chicken portions, skinned and each cut into 2	400 g (14 oz) can chickpeas, drained, or 125 g (4½ oz) cooked chickpeas
2 small onions, each weighing about 100 g (3½ oz), quartered	1 tablespoon tomato purée
2 medium carrots, cut into 2.5 cm (1 inch) chunks	salt and freshly ground black pepper
75 g (3 oz) green beans, cut into 2.5 cm (1 inch) pieces	225 g (8 oz) couscous
500 ml (18 fl oz) chicken stock	1 large tomato, skinned (see page 33), deseeded and chopped, to garnish
2 teaspoons each of ground turmeric, ground coriander and ground cumin	fresh coriander leaves, to garnish

Heat the oil in a large, heavy-bottomed saucepan or flameproof casserole (see note), add the chicken pieces, and cook until browned. Add the onion pieces, the carrots and green beans, the stock, spices and raisins, and simmer for 30 minutes or until the chicken and onions are tender.

Add the chickpeas to the pan, and tomato purée, season with salt and pepper, and stir. Bring back to a simmer. Remove 4–5 tablespoons liquid from the pan and reserve. Add the couscous to the pan, stir, cover and turn off the heat, but leave the pan on the hob. Check after 5 minutes, adding a little extra stock or water if all is absorbed. After 20 minutes the couscous should be ready.

Stir gently and serve with a little of the reserved liquid spooned over each serving, and garnished with tomato and coriander.

NOTES AND TIPS

✦ *This method of cooking couscous depends upon a heavy, heat-retaining cooking pan, and it helps if you cook on a solid hot plate. If the couscous has cooled too much by the time it is ready to serve, add a little extra liquid to the pan, and heat very gently for 5 minutes.*

NUTRITION

CALORIES PER PORTION: 510	PROTEIN: ★★★ FIBRE: ★★ CARBOHYDRATE: ★★★
TOTAL FAT PER PORTION: 13 g	VITAMINS: B_3, B_6, E, C, beta-carotene
SATURATED FAT PER PORTION: 2.5 g	MINERALS: K, Mg, Ca, Fe, Zn

Salmon Rice Supper

SERVES 4

NOT everyone likes spicy rice dishes so this creamy recipe makes a nice change. It's also good served as a salad. Don't be surprised to find that real cream cheese is one of the ingredients – as I've told you before, healthy eating doesn't mean banning foods, but achieving a sensible balance.

375 g (12 oz) salmon fillet	salt (optional)
1 tablespoon corn oil	150 g (5½ oz) 8 per cent fat fromage frais
1 large red pepper, deseeded and cut into 2.5 cm (1 inch) diamonds	1 tablespoon cream cheese
	2 tablespoons freshly grated Parmesan cheese
1 medium courgette	1 teaspoon Dijon mustard
1 large leek, thinly sliced	a little skimmed milk
225 g (8 oz) mixed long-grain and wild rice	chopped fresh parsley, to garnish
825 ml (1½ pints) fish or vegetable stock	
100 g (3½ oz) small mushrooms, sliced	

Cut the salmon into bite-sized chunks and poach for 1–2 minutes in water. Drain and set aside.

Heat the oil in a large non-stick frying pan, add the red pepper and stir-fry for 1 minute. Cut the courgette lengthways in quarters, then into 2.5 cm (1 inch) pieces. Add to the pan with the leek, and stir-fry for a few minutes or until the vegetables are *al dente*.

Add the rice, stir, and add the stock. Simmer for 15 minutes, then stir in the mushrooms. Simmer for a further 2 minutes. Taste the rice and add a little salt if you like. (If the rice looks too dry, add a little more water or stock.)

Return the salmon to the pan, but don't stir. Beat together the fromage frais, cream cheese, Parmesan and mustard, thinning with a little milk to a sauce consistency. Pour this over the salmon rice and fork through just to mix very lightly. Serve garnished with chopped parsley.

NOTES AND TIPS

✦ *You could use canned salmon instead of fresh.*

NUTRITION

CALORIES PER PORTION: 490	PROTEIN: ★★★ FIBRE: ★★ CARBOHYDRATE: ★★
TOTAL FAT PER PORTION: 22 g	VITAMINS: B group, beta-carotene, C, E, D
SATURATED FAT PER PORTION: 6.5 g	MINERALS: Zn, Ca, K, Fe, Mg

CHAPTER 9

SALADS

Not so long ago, you either loved salad or you hated it – and most people hated it! That was because 'salad' was almost always the same – a limp offering of butterhead lettuce leaves, three slices of cucumber, three slices of tasteless tomato and a small dollop of salad cream (if you were lucky). These days, a salad can be – and often is – anything you want it to be: starter, main course, side dish; light and delicate; robust and hearty. It doesn't even have to be cold, or full of mostly raw ingredients. No wonder, today, we are becoming a nation of salad-lovers.

I am a great fan of all-in-one salads that provide you with protein, carbohydrate, vitamins, minerals, fibre, fruit and vegetables all in the same plateful. Which is what this chapter is mostly about.

When making your own salad for a main meal or lunch, remember that for a balanced meal it should include:

◆ raw vegetables and fruit;

◆ a protein source – e.g nuts, cheese, egg, chicken, fish, beans;

◆ carbohydrate – rice or grains, potato, pasta, or bread, for instance.

If you dress your salad in a heavy, fat-laden dressing, such as full-fat mayonnaise, you will spoil part of the good, fresh, low-calorie appeal of your salad. Instead try any of those I've used on the salads in the pages that follow, or else simply use a juice, or a vinegar, or even one of the commercial fat-free dressings. Or try my trick of mixing a high-fat dressing, such as mayonnaise, with low-fat natural yogurt for the best of both worlds.

Nutrition Notes

Not all salad items are high in vitamin C (or indeed any vitamins) or fibre. That's because some are almost all water so their nutrients are, literally, very 'diluted'.

Best sources of vitamin C for use in salads are: citrus fruits, peppers, parsley, Chinese leaves, cabbage, spinach, watercress, tomatoes, mangos, melon, pineapple and bananas. Most salad vegetables and fruits are low in fat and calories, so you can eat them freely.

For more nutrition, fat and calorie information on cheeses, nuts and pulses, see pages 91–2. For more on meats, chicken and fish, see pages 43, 61 and 77. And for more on fruits, see page 133. For additional vegetables, see page 92.

CALORIE AND FAT COUNTS FOR SALAD INGREDIENTS AND DRESSINGS

Salad vegetables, per 25 g (1 oz) unless otherwise stated

	Cals	Fat (grams)
Artichoke hearts, each	10	trace
Asparagus spears, each	5	trace
Avocado	48	5.0
Beansprouts	7	trace
Beetroot	11	trace
Celery, 1 stalk	2	trace
Chicory	2	trace
Chinese leaves	3	trace
Cucumber	2	trace
Lettuce	3	trace
Mustard and cress, 1 punnet	5	trace
Onion	6	trace
Pepper, green	3	trace
Pepper, red	8	trace
Radish, 1	2	trace
Tomato, 1 medium	7	trace
Watercress	3	trace

Salad fruits, all per fruit unless otherwise stated

Apple, dessert	45	trace
Apricot, dried, per 25 g (1 oz)	45	trace
Apricot, fresh	10	trace
Date, fresh or dried	15	trace
Grapes, per 25 g (1 oz)	16	trace
Mango	100	trace
Melon, 200 g (7 oz) slice, peeled weight	38	0.2
Orange	50	trace
Raisins, sultanas, per 25 g (1 oz)	62	trace

Miscellaneous salad ingredients, per tablespoon unless otherwise stated

Anchovies, each	10	0.7
Olives, each	3	0.3
Sun-dried tomatoes, each	15	1.5

table continues

	Cals	**Fat (grams)**
Capers	2	trace
Cannellini beans	20	trace
Pine nuts	42	4.2
Sesame seeds	50	4.8
Sunflower seeds	48	4.0
Croûtons, baked (my recipe, see page 127), per 25 g (1 oz) portion	55	2.0
Croûtons, fried, 25 g (1 oz)	145	10.0

Dressings, per tablespoon

	Cals	Fat
Creamy Dressing (see page 130)	21	1.7
Fromage frais, 8 per cent	15	1.0
Juices, e.g. orange, lime	5	trace
Mayonnaise, full-fat	120	12.0
Mayonnaise, reduced-fat (e.g. Hellmann's)	45	4.5
Mayonnaise, 70 per cent fat-free (e.g. Kraft)	18	1.4
Olive oil	135	15.0
Salad cream	56	5.0
Vinaigrette, (French dressing)	100	11.0
Vinaigrette, light (see page 123)	50	5.0
Vinaigrette, oil-free (e.g. Waistline)	2–6	trace
Vinegar, all	trace	—
Yogurt, natural, low-fat	8	trace

Prawn, Rice and Avocado Salad

SERVES 4

I DON'T use brown rice all the time, but in salads it does have a nice, nutty flavour that goes especially well with avocado. This salad is packed with vitamin E and zinc.

salt and freshly ground black pepper	325 g (12 oz) cooked peeled prawns (or leave a few unpeeled, if fresh)
225 g (8 oz) easy-cook brown rice	1 small green pepper, deseeded and finely chopped
1 sachet saffron strands	
1 large ripe avocado (or 2 small)	6 medium spring onions, chopped
juice of 1 lime or ½ lemon	15 g (½ oz) pine nuts
2 tablespoons good olive oil	2 medium tomatoes, deseeded and chopped
2 tablespoons good red wine vinegar	fresh parsley, to garnish
1 teaspoon Dijon mustard	
1 teaspoon brown sugar	

Pour 500 ml (18 fl oz) water into a large saucepan, salt lightly and bring to the boil. Add the rice and saffron, and cook for 20 minutes or for the time specified on the rice packet. Drain the rice and leave to cool slightly.

Meanwhile, halve, stone, peel and slice the avocado, and coat with the lime or lemon juice to prevent browning. Make a dressing by combining the oil, vinegar, 2 tablespoons cold water, the mustard and sugar in a bowl. Season with a little salt and plenty of black pepper.

When the rice is just warm, add the avocado and all the remaining ingredients (except any unpeeled prawns and the parsley) and toss in the dressing. Garnish with unpeeled prawns, if using, and parsley.

NOTES AND TIPS

✦ *You can add a pinch of curry powder to the dressing if you like.*
✦ *Vegetarians can use 50 g (2 oz) almonds instead of the prawns.*
✦ *Fresh cooked prawns are best in this recipe, but if you have to use frozen, make sure they are of good quality with a low water content.*

NUTRITION

CALORIES PER PORTION: 490	PROTEIN: ★★★ FIBRE: ★★ CARBOHYDRATE: ★★
TOTAL FAT PER PORTION: 23 g	VITAMINS: B$_3$, folic acid, E, C, beta-carotene
SATURATED FAT PER PORTION: 5 g	MINERALS: Mg, K, Zn, Ca

Pasta, Tuna and Pepper Salad

SERVES 4

A GOOD lunch for slimmers, this is very filling for few calories, and contains a wealth of almost all the vitamins and minerals known to man – and woman!

150 g (5½ oz) dried pasta shapes (e.g. shells)	1 large red pepper, deseeded and chopped
125 ml (4½ fl oz) fat-free 1000-Island-style dressing	7.5 cm (3 inch) piece of cucumber, chopped
100 g (3½ oz) low-fat natural Bio yogurt	2 small celery stalks, chopped
75 ml (3 fl oz) skimmed milk	4 medium spring onions, chopped
pinch of caster sugar	50 g (2 oz) sweetcorn kernels, cooked
a little lemon juice	1 green-skinned apple
salt and freshly ground black pepper	pretty lettuce leaves, e.g. oak leaf and frisée
400 g (14 oz) can tuna in brine or water, drained	chopped fresh parsley and paprika, to garnish

Cook the pasta in plenty of lightly salted boiling water until *al dente* (don't overcook). Drain and tip into a large mixing bowl.

Mix together the 1000-Island dressing, yogurt, milk, sugar and lemon juice, and season with a little salt and plenty of black pepper.

Flake the tuna on to the pasta. Add all the chopped vegetables and the sweetcorn. Core and chop the apple and add to the bowl with the dressing. Pile the salad into a serving bowl or bowls lined with lettuce leaves, and garnish with parsley and paprika.

NUTRITION

CALORIES PER PORTION: 335   PROTEIN: ★★★ FIBRE: ★★ CARBOHYDRATE: ★★★
TOTAL FAT PER PORTION: 2 g   VITAMINS: B group, D, C, beta-carotene
SATURATED FAT PER PORTION: 0.5 g   MINERALS: K, Mg, Fe, Zn, Ca

---

Pasta, Bacon and Apple Crunch

SERVES 4

THIS simple salad works because the fruit acts as the perfect foil to the bacon's saltiness.

175 g (6 oz) pasta 'spirals' (fusilli), half verde, half white	4 tablespoons wine vinegar
	1 teaspoon Dijon mustard
100 g (3½ oz) small broccoli florets	1 teaspoon brown sugar
120 g (4½ oz) prosciutto (about 8 slices)	1 large red apple
4 tablespoons olive oil	100 g (3½ oz) cantaloupe melon, cubed

Cook the pasta in lightly salted boiling water until *al dente*, then drain. Parboil the broccoli for 3 minutes, then drain. Cut the ham into bite-sized pieces and grill until crisp.

Make a dressing by beating together the olive oil, wine vinegar, 2 tablespoons cold water, the mustard and sugar. Season with salt and pepper. Core and chop the apple and toss with the melon and broccoli in the dressing. Toss with the pasta, then arrange in serving bowls and top with the prosciutto.

NOTES AND TIPS
✦ *Ordinary lean back bacon can be used instead of the prosciutto, if preferred.*

NUTRITION

CALORIES PER PORTION: 430   PROTEIN: ★★ FIBRE: ★★ CARBOHYDRATE: ★★
TOTAL FAT PER PORTION: 28 g   VITAMINS: B group, beta-carotene, C
SATURATED FAT PER PORTION: 7 g   MINERALS: K, Fe, Mg, Zn, Ca

Smoked Turkey and Mango Salad with Bagels

SERVES 4

HERE'S a taste of New York in this pretty salad that's easy to put together and high in beta-carotene, C and E vitamins, as well as zinc and iron.

1 radicchio	2 tablespoons low-fat natural Bio yogurt
1 green lettuce	2 tablespoons cranberry sauce
12 slices of smoked turkey, each weighing about 25 g (1 oz)	1 teaspoon lemon juice
	good bunch of watercress, to garnish
1 large ripe mango	4 bagels, each weighing about 75 g (3 oz), to serve
3 tablespoons reduced-fat mayonnaise	

Arrange the radicchio and green lettuce leaves on serving plates with the turkey slices to one side. Peel and slice the mango, and divide the slices between the plates.

In a small bowl, mix together the mayonnaise, yogurt, cranberry sauce and lemon juice, and divide this, too, between the plates. Remove the toughest stalks from the watercress and garnish each plate with some sprigs. Serve with the bagels.

NOTES AND TIPS
✦ *Spread your bagels with a little low-salt butter or low-fat spread, if you like. Butter adds 45 calories and 5 g fat per portion; low-fat spread about 20 calories and 2 g fat per portion.*

NUTRITION

CALORIES PER PORTION: 415   PROTEIN: ★★★ FIBRE: ★★ CARBOHYDRATE: ★★★
TOTAL FAT PER PORTION: 6.5 g   VITAMINS: beta-carotene, C, E, B_3, folic acid
SATURATED FAT PER PORTION: 2.5 g   MINERALS: Zn, Fe, K, Ca

Seafood Salad with Oriental Dressing

SERVES 4

REALLY rich in vitamins and minerals, this 'stir-fry' salad makes an excellent slimmer's meal. Although it's filling, it is low in carbohydrates, so have plenty of bread, rice, potatoes, pasta and so on for the other meal of the day.

1 clove garlic, peeled and very finely chopped	100 g (3½ oz) Chinese leaves (see note)
1 tablespoon groundnut oil	100 g (3½ oz) beansprouts
1 tablespoon sesame oil	1 red pepper, deseeded and sliced
2 tablespoons sherry vinegar (or wine vinegar, but see note)	40 g (1½ oz) mangetout, blanched
	4 spring onions, chopped
1 tablespoon soy sauce	4 giant cooked prawns, with tails on
1 teaspoon Tabasco sauce	1 tablespoon sesame seeds, to garnish
400 g (14 oz) frozen mixed seafood, thawed	
75 g (3 oz) medium egg thread noodles	

In a bowl, blend together the garlic, two oils, vinegar, soy sauce and Tabasco. Add the mixed seafood and leave for 30 minutes.

Transfer the seafood mixture to a small saucepan and cook for 2 minutes, then set aside. Cook or soak the noodles in boiling water according to the packet instructions, then drain.

Arrange the Chinese leaves in a serving bowl or bowls. Combine the seafood mixture and noodles in a mixing bowl, and add the beansprouts, red pepper, mangetout and spring onions. Place in the serving bowl(s) and add a giant prawn for each person. Garnish with the sesame seeds.

NOTES AND TIPS
✦ *If you haven't any Chinese leaves, Cos lettuce will do.*
✦ *Sherry vinegar is particularly nice in dressings with an Oriental feel.*

NUTRITION

CALORIES PER PORTION: 300   PROTEIN: ★★★ FIBRE: ★★ CARBOHYDRATE: ★
TOTAL FAT PER PORTION: 11.5 g   VITAMINS: B group, C, beta-carotene, E
SATURATED FAT PER PORTION: 2 g   MINERALS: Fe, Mg, K, Zn

Salade Maison with French Bread

SERVES 4

I FIRST had this typically French salad in a holiday cottage in Wales, of all places. The French owner of the complex was a wonderful chef and, luckily, would cook delicious meals to order for guests. Her husband would run across the courtyard carrying the food under silver domes to ensure we ate before the food got cold – which was just as well, as Salade Maison definitely needs to be served warm. Lovely holidays, lovely food, bliss!

100 g (3½ oz) lean, low-salt back bacon	a little olive oil
4 slices of French bread, about 200 g (7 oz) in all	1 clove garlic, peeled and halved
1 pack of mixed crisp salad leaves	**For the dressing**
2 teaspoons olive oil	2 tablespoons olive oil
12 chicken livers, halved, if large, and soaked in a little milk, then drained	2 teaspoons balsamic vinegar
1 clove garlic, peeled and chopped	1 tablespoon red wine vinegar
For the croûtons	1 teaspoon Dijon mustard
2 slices of bread, crusts removed	pinch of brown sugar
	salt and freshly ground black pepper

To make the croûtons, brush the bread slices with a little olive oil and rub with the clove of garlic. Cut into bite-sized cubes and bake in the oven at 190°C/375°F/Gas Mark 5 until golden and crisp. Keep warm.

Chop the bacon into bite-sized pieces and grill or dry-fry until crisp. Keep warm. To make the dressing, beat together the olive oil, two vinegars, mustard and sugar. Season with salt and pepper. (Put the French bread in the oven to warm if you like.)

Tip the salad leaves into a serving bowl or bowls. Heat the 2 teaspoons olive oil in a non-stick frying pan, add the chicken livers and garlic, and stir-fry over a high heat for about 2 minutes. Add the bacon to the pan and stir-fry for a few seconds, then toss the livers, garlic and bacon into the salad leaves. Pour the salad dressing into the frying pan and swirl round for a few seconds to warm, then pour that, too, over the salad. Sprinkle the croûtons over and serve immediately with the French bread.

NUTRITION

CALORIES PER PORTION (INCLUDING FRENCH BREAD): 380
TOTAL FAT PER PORTION: 19 g
SATURATED FAT PER PORTION: 4.5 g

PROTEIN: ★★★ FIBRE: ★ CARBOHYDRATE: ★★
VITAMINS: A, B group, E, C
MINERALS: Fe, Zn, K, Ca

Note: Pregnant women should avoid liver because of its potentially toxic levels of vitamin A. This dish contains 207 mg cholesterol per portion.

Tuna and Artichoke Salad

SERVES 4

I INVENTED this salad one day through necessity, using what I had in the storecupboard for an unexpected lunch. It's a bit like a salad niçoise. I was very pleased with the way it turned out.

400 g (14 oz) can tuna in brine or water, drained	2 tablespoons white wine vinegar
half 400 g (14 oz) can artichoke hearts	salt and freshly ground black pepper
2 round lettuces	pinch of mustard powder
1 large or 2 medium tomatoes, chopped	pinch of sugar
half 400 g (14 oz) can cannellini beans, drained and rinsed	**For the garnish**
	16 black olives, stoned
2–3 shallots, peeled and sliced into rings	8 capers, drained
For the dressing	fresh parsley
2 tablespoons olive oil	

Flake the tuna into big chunks and drain the artichoke hearts well, then pat dry with kitchen paper. Wash the lettuces, if necessary, peel off the outer leaves and arrange them in a salad bowl or bowls. Cut the two lettuce hearts into eight wedges and arrange these in the bowl(s), too. Add the tuna, artichokes, tomatoes, beans and shallots. Mix together all the dressing ingredients and pour over the salad. Garnish with the olives, capers and parsley.

NOTES AND TIPS

✦ *You can add a hard-boiled egg or two to the salad if you like. Each egg adds 80 calories, 6 g fat and 250 mg cholesterol.*

✦ *Asparagus tips and green beans would be nice additions or replacements in this dish.*

✦ *Because this salad is quite low in carbohydrate, serve it with some crusty bread.*

NUTRITION

CALORIES PER PORTION: 245   PROTEIN: ★★★ FIBRE: ★★ CARBOHYDRATE: ★
TOTAL FAT PER PORTION: 10 g   VITAMINS: D, E, beta-carotene, C
SATURATED FAT PER PORTION: 1.5 g   MINERALS: K, Mg, Fe, Zn, Ca

---

OPPOSITE   Salmon Rice Supper (page 119)

Potato and Pepperoni Salad

SERVES 4

I ADORE cold new potatoes, and they are a perfect foil for slices of spicy sausage. Potatoes, especially when young, have a surprisingly high vitamin-C content, and plenty of fibre and protein, too.

900 g (2 lb) new potatoes, scrubbed	**For the dressing**
salt	6 tablespoons oil-free French dressing
90 g (3½ oz) pack ready-sliced pepperoni (see note)	1 tablespoon olive oil
	1 teaspoon Dijon mustard
12 cherry tomatoes	1 teaspoon chopped fresh mint
50 g (2 oz) cucumber	1 tablespoon chopped fresh parsley
100 g (3½ oz) sweetcorn kernels	1 teaspoon brown sugar
salad leaves, to serve	

Cook the potatoes in lightly salted boiling water until tender. Meanwhile, grill or dry-fry the pepperoni until a little crisp. Carefully slice the cherry tomatoes in half, and cut the cucumber into small chunks. Cook the sweetcorn kernels in boiling water until tender. Drain the potatoes and sweetcorn.

To make the dressing, beat together the oil-free French dressing, the olive oil, mustard, mint, parsley and sugar. In a large bowl, combine the dressing with the potatoes, pepperoni and vegetables.

Serve on the salad leaves.

NOTES AND TIPS

✦ *You can use ham or smoked tofu in the salad instead of the pepperoni. You should be able to find 90 g (3½ oz) packs of sliced pepperoni in the chilled cabinet at the supermarket.*

✦ *You can try the salad using a creamy dressing of half low-fat yogurt, half low-fat mayonnaise with a little mustard, which would be similar in calories and fat.*

NUTRITION

CALORIES PER PORTION: 320	PROTEIN: ★★ FIBRE: ★★ CARBOHYDRATE: ★★★
TOTAL FAT PER PORTION: 13 g	VITAMINS: C, beta-carotene, E
SATURATED FAT PER PORTION: 3.5 g	MINERALS: K

OPPOSITE   Braised Peaches with Strawberry Fool (page 139), Brown Bread Ice Cream with Apricot Sauce (page 143)

Waldorf Salad in Pasta Shells

SERVES 4

LIKE all nuts, walnuts are high in fat, but it is the unsaturated kind that is good for you, and they contain lots of vitamin E. This salad is very filling and pretty – ideal for lunch guests. Alternatively, half portions make a nice starter before a low-fat main course.

20 dried jumbo pasta shells, (about 110 g/4 oz)	celery leaves, to garnish
salt	**For the dressing**
curly endive or frisée leaves	4 tablespoons low-fat mayonnaise
1 head of chicory	4 tablespoons low-fat natural Bio yogurt
1 large red apple	2 tablespoons skimmed milk
50 g (2 oz) sultanas	1 teaspoon mustard powder
100 g (3½ oz) walnut halves, each cut into 2	1 teaspoon lemon juice
1 celery stalk, thinly sliced	salt and freshly ground black pepper
150 g (5½ oz) medium-fat goat's cheese	

To make the dressing, combine the mayonnaise, yogurt, milk, mustard and lemon juice, and season with salt and pepper.

Cook the pasta shells in lightly salted boiling water for about 15 minutes or until *al dente*. Drain. Arrange the frisée or endive leaves around serving plates and arrange five chicory leaves on each plate.

Core and chop the apple, and add it to the dressing so that it doesn't brown. Add the sultanas, walnuts and celery to the dressing. Cut the goat's cheese into 20 small pieces and stir gently into the dressing.

Fill each pasta shell with a spoonful of salad, and put each filled shell on to a chicory leaf. Garnish each shell with a little celery leaf.

NOTES AND TIPS

✦ *You could use various other medium- or low-fat cheeses in this salad, such as feta or half-fat Edam.*

✦ *The goat's cheese is quite soft but it will just about cut, and if you mix it gently into the salad it won't disintegrate. It has a very special fresh flavour that no other cheese quite matches.*

NUTRITION

CALORIES PER PORTION: 460	PROTEIN: ★★★ FIBRE: ★★ CARBOHYDRATE: ★
TOTAL FAT PER PORTION: 26 g	VITAMINS: B group, E, C
SATURATED FAT PER PORTION: 6.5 g	MINERALS: K, Mg, Fe, Zn, Ca

Curried Rice Salad with Chicken and Bananas

SERVES 4

HAWAII meets India for an unusual salad combination that I invented to use up some left-over chicken and pineapple pieces!

225 g (8 oz) brown rice	1 small green pepper, deseeded and chopped
salt	4 teaspoons sweet mango chutney
1 teaspoon curry powder	2 tablespoons reduced-fat mayonnaise
4 tablespoons coconut milk	275 g (10 oz) cooked chicken meat (no skin or bone)
1 quantity dressing (see page 129)	
2 medium bananas	1 pack of mixed salad leaves
100 g (3½ oz) pineapple pieces (see note)	chopped fresh coriander or parsley, to garnish

Cook the rice in lightly salted boiling water with the curry powder and half the coconut milk until tender. Drain and cool. Meanwhile, make up the dressing as described on page 129.

When the rice has cooled a little, peel the bananas and chop into small chunks. Combine with the dressing, pineapple pieces, green pepper and rice.

Combine the chutney, remaining coconut milk and low-fat mayonnaise in a bowl, and add the chicken, tossing to coat well. Arrange the salad leaves around the edge of four serving plates, then arrange the rice inside them in a small ring. Fill the centre with the chicken mixture and garnish with coriander or parsley.

NOTES AND TIPS

✦ *You could also use leftover turkey meat in this dish.*
✦ *You can use fresh pineapple or well-drained canned pineapple in juice.*

NUTRITION

CALORIES PER PORTION: 425	PROTEIN: ★★★ FIBRE: ★★ CARBOHYDRATE: ★★★
TOTAL FAT PER PORTION: 12 g	VITAMINS: B group, E
SATURATED FAT PER PORTION: 4.5 g	MINERALS: Mg, Zn, Fe, K

CHAPTER 10

DESERTS

Many people feel guilty about enjoying a dessert after a meal, and it is true that very many of the traditional puddings, pies and confections are likely to be higher in both fat and calories than the course they follow, and not something to be indulged in more than very occasionally if you care at all about your waistline.

However, if you cook clever, you **can** enjoy ices, crumbles, pancakes, brûlées – all manner of sweet things, in fact – without guilt. My favourite desserts – a selection of which appears in this chapter – are either based on traditional fare, but with half the fat, or else they are new inventions. Either way, I absolutely love cooking up things that taste wicked but aren't! My puddings are not only low, or reasonably low, in both fat and calories, but they also all have something positive to offer, nutritionally speaking. I won't offer a dessert, however fat-free or slimming it might be, unless it is also a worthwhile source of vitamins or calcium, fibre, iron – or whatever.

So how have I made delicious-sounding desserts healthy? Here are some of the methods I've used that you can copy at home:

✦ I've used fructose instead of sugar most of the time. Fructose is a natural fruit sugar with the same number of calories as sugar (sucrose) but it is twice as sweet, so you only have to use half the amount. Another advantage of fructose is that it doesn't promote such a rapid rise in blood sugar levels as sucrose, so it helps prevent the 'rebound hunger' that often occurs after a high-sugar snack.

✦ I've used naturally sweet foods, such as dried fruit and bananas, instead of adding sweetness, wherever possible.

✦ I never use a full-fat dairy product when a lower-fat one will do just as well. Instead of double cream, I use half-fat crème fraîche, for instance; I always use low-fat Greek yogurt instead of the full-fat kind; I choose fromage frais instead of mascarpone cheese; I use low-calorie ice cream instead of the full-fat sort. And so on. You'll see just how many calories and how much fat you save by checking through the 'dairy' list below.

✦ If I use pastry, I always use filo instead of puff or shortcrust. With filo, you *add* the fat, so you can just brush on a little oil, saving masses of fat and calories when compared with ordinary pastry.

Nutrition Notes

Get as much fruit as you can into your desserts, for their vitamin C and fibre content. Milk and dairy products in desserts will provide calcium.

Use wholemeal flour as often as you can when flour is called for, for its added fibre and B vitamins. Choose oats for a crumble topping as they are high in soluble fibre (see page 11). Nuts are a good source of vitamin E but are very high in fat, so if you're weight-watching, don't go overboard. Sugar contains no nutrients, and neither does syrup, so use sparingly and replace with fructose or natural sweeteners when you can.

Use the following table of fat and calorie counts to help you make wise choices when you feel the urge for something sweet after your meal!

FAT AND CALORIE COUNTS FOR DESSERTS AND ACCOMPANIMENTS

Fruits, per item unless otherwise stated

	Cals	Fat (grams)
(For more fruits, see page 121)		
Apple, cooking, per 25 g (1 oz)	10	trace
Banana, medium	80	trace
Blackberries per 25 g (1 oz)	7	trace
Blackcurrants, per 25 g (1 oz)	7	trace
Cherries, 25 g (1 oz)	10	trace
Damsons, 25 g (1 oz)	8	trace
Fig, fresh	10	trace
Grapefruit, half	20	trace
Kiwi fruit	25	trace
Lemon	20	trace
Nectarine	50	trace
Peach, pear	50	trace
Pineapple, one ring	25	trace
Plum	20	trace
Prune	10	trace
Raspberries	6	trace
Rhubarb, 25 g (1 oz)	2	trace
Satsuma	20	trace
Strawberries, 25 g (1 oz)	6	trace
Sultanas, 25 g (1 oz)	62	trace

Carbohydrates, per 25 g (1 oz)

Oats, rolled	94	2.3
Flour, white	85	0.3
Flour, wholemeal	77	0.5

Dairy, per 25 ml (1 fl oz) unless otherwise stated

(For cheeses, see page 91)

	Cals	Fat (grams)
Butter	184	20.4
Cream, double	112	12.0
Cream, Shape Double	58	5.5
Cream, single	53	5.3
Cream, Shape Single	27	2.0
Cream, whipping	93	9.8
Cream, half-fat	37	3.3
Crème fraîche, full-fat	98	10.2
Crème fraîche, low-fat	42	3.7
Custard, standard	24	0.75
Custard, low-fat	18	0.35
Egg, 1 size-3	80	6.0
Fromage frais, 8 per cent fat	28	2.0
Fromage frais, fat-free	13	trace
Milk, full-fat	16	1.0
Milk, skimmed	8	trace
Yogurt, low-fat natural	14	0.2
Yogurt, Greek	33	2.2
Yogurt, Greek, low-fat	20	1.25

Sweeteners all per 1 tablespoon

Sugar	60	—
Fructose	40	—
Honey	44	—
Treacle	50	—
Syrup	45	—
Artificial sprinkler	6	—

Miscellaneous, per 25 g (1 oz) unless otherwise stated

Chocolate (milk, plain or white)	132	7.5
Chopped nuts	152	13.5
Flaked or ground almonds	153	14.0
Desiccated coconut	151	15.5
Low-fat spread	97	10.0
Wine, sweet, 100 ml (3½ fl oz)	94	—

Apricot and Nut Crumble

SERVES 4–6

A TRADITIONAL crumble topping contains butter, flour and sugar in roughly equal proportions, and the fruit filling normally has another 75 g (3 oz) sugar or so. The fruit in my crumble is naturally sweet so there's no need for added sugar. And the topping is really rather good for you with its oats, seeds and nuts. My kids adore it, so give it a try! It's also very high in fibre, iron and vitamin E, by the way.

200 g (7 oz) ready-to-eat dried apricots	75 g (3 oz) porridge oats
2 medium bananas	1 tablespoon golden syrup
4 tablespoons lemon juice	25 g (1 oz) low-salt butter
25 g (1 oz) chopped nuts	1 tablespoon dark brown sugar
1 tablespoon sunflower seeds	

Simmer the apricots in enough water just to cover for 30 minutes (or microwave in water for 15 minutes on medium). Meanwhile, peel and slice the bananas and put in the base of a 825 ml (1½ pint) soufflé dish. Spoon the lemon juice over them. Drain the apricots, reserving the cooking water. Spoon the apricots on top of the bananas, and add 4 tablespoons of the apricot cooking water.

Mix together the nuts, seeds and oats in a bowl. Melt the syrup, butter and sugar in a small saucepan, and stir into the oat mixture until the dry mix is well coated. Spoon this evenly over the apricots and smooth down. Bake in the oven at 190°C/375°F/Gas Mark 5 for 20–25 minutes or until the top is golden.

NOTES AND TIPS

◆ *You could use plums instead of the apricots – 400 g (14 oz) stoned red or Victoria plums would be about right.*

NUTRITION

CALORIES PER PORTION: 338 (4 servings); 225 (6 servings)

TOTAL FAT PER PORTION: 12 g (4 servings); 8 g (6 servings)

SATURATED FAT PER PORTION: 4 g (4 servings); 2.7 g (6 servings)

PROTEIN: ★ FIBRE: ★★★

CARBOHYDRATE: ★★★

VITAMINS: beta-carotene, B group, E, A

MINERALS: Zn, K, Fe, Mg, Ca

Bananas Suzette

SERVES 4

A WEIGHT-WATCHERS' version of comfort pudding! Bananas are a good source of magnesium and potassium, and are quite high in vitamin C and fibre.

2 teaspoons sunflower oil	juice of 1 orange
15 g (½ oz) low-salt butter	25 ml (1 fl oz) Cointreau or Grand Marnier
4 large bananas	4 teaspoons brown sugar

Heat the oil and butter in a frying pan. Peel the bananas and slice each diagonally into four. Add the slices to the pan and fry over a medium heat until just turning golden. Add the rest of the ingredients and bubble for 1–2 minutes. Serve each portion of bananas with the pan juices poured over.

NOTES AND TIPS

✦ *The bananas are nice with low-fat Greek yogurt at 15 calories and less than 1 g of fat per tablespoon.*
✦ *If you're feeling festive you can flame the pan with a tablespoon of warm brandy before serving.*
✦ *If you like, you can add some orange segments to the pan, too, for extra vitamin C.*

NUTRITION

CALORIES PER PORTION: 225   PROTEIN: ★ FIBRE: ★★ CARBOHYDRATE: ★★★
TOTAL FAT PER PORTION: 6 g   VITAMINS: C, A
SATURATED FAT PER PORTION: 2.5 g   MINERALS: K, Mg

Exotic Fruits Brûlée

SERVES 4

TRADITIONAL cream or custard brûlée is a very high-fat treat indeed. Using half-fat crème fraîche and lots of fresh fruit, we can turn a nutritional disaster into something you can enjoy occasionally without guilt!

400 g (14 oz) prepared exotic fruits, e.g. 100 g (3½ oz) sliced mango, 100 g (3½ oz) sliced paw paw, 2 sliced kiwi fruits (50 g/2 oz each), 25 g (1 oz) passion fruit pulp, and 75 g (3 oz) pineapple pieces	300 ml (11 fl oz) half-fat crème fraîche
	100 g (3½ oz) light brown sugar (demerara)

Heat the grill to its hottest for several minutes. Meanwhile, arrange the fruit in the bottom of four ramekin dishes. Smooth the crème fraîche over the top to cover completely and level the surface. Sprinkle the sugar on top very evenly so that it completely covers the crème.

Place the ramekins under the grill, near the heat, until the sugar has caramelised (melted and turned a dark brown colour). Immediately remove from the heat and place in the fridge for 1 hour, by which time the tops of the brûlées should be hard.

NOTES AND TIPS

✦ *If the grill isn't really hot, the crème may bubble up through the sugar before the sugar melts.*
✦ *You can't use fructose in this dish; it has to be sugar.*
✦ *In midsummer, this is delicious made with strawberries, peaches and bananas.*

NUTRITION

CALORIES PER PORTION: 275
TOTAL FAT PER PORTION: 11 g
SATURATED FAT PER PORTION: 7.5 g

PROTEIN: ★ FIBRE: ★★ CARBOHYDRATE: ★★★
VITAMINS: C, beta-carotene
MINERALS: K

Strawberry and Peach Layer

SERVES 4

A QUICK summer dessert, high in vitamin C and calcium.

300 g (11 oz) 8 per cent fat fromage frais	2 ripe peaches
4 teaspoons icing sugar	225 g (8 oz) strawberries
a very little skimmed milk	

Beat the fromage frais with half the sugar and a very little skimmed milk to give the consistency of lightly whipped cream. Peel, stone and chop the peaches. Hull and chop the strawberries, if large, retaining four whole strawberries for decoration.

Spoon a little of the fromage frais into each of four wine or sundae glasses. Divide the chopped strawberries evenly between the glasses and sprinkle a little of the remaining icing sugar over each. Spoon in more fromage frais, then a layer of peaches. Finally, top with the rest of the fromage frais. Decorate with strawberries and chill for 1 hour before serving.

NUTRITION

CALORIES PER PORTION: 150
TOTAL FAT PER PORTION: 6 g
SATURATED FAT PER PORTION: 4 g

PROTEIN: ★★★ FIBRE: ★★ CARBOHYDRATE: ★★
VITAMINS: C
MINERALS: Ca

Raspberry Ice

MAKES **8** 125 ml (4½ fl oz) Scoops

AN AVERAGE scoop of luxury ice cream is 250 calories. This ice contains half that with the bonus of vitamin C, and many people swear by cranberry juice as a cure-all. Whether it is or not, it still makes a good ice, so eat and enjoy!

450 g (1 lb) raspberries, fresh or thawed frozen	100 ml (3½ oz) fruit sugar (fructose)
150 ml (5½ fl oz) orange juice	225 g (8 oz) 8 per cent fat fromage frais
125 ml (4½ fl oz) cranberry or cranberry and raspberry juice or all orange juice	1 teaspoon lemon juice

Purée the raspberries in a blender or food processor, then sieve them if you prefer to remove the pips. Mix with the rest of the ingredients. Freeze in an ice cream maker, or put in a plastic container and freeze in the freezer for about 5 hours, beating once or twice during this time to break down large ice crystals. Remove from the freezer a few minutes before serving.

NUTRITION

CALORIES PER PORTION (ONE 125 ML/4½ FL OZ SCOOP): 105
TOTAL FAT PER PORTION: 5 g
SATURATED FAT PER PORTION: 3 g

PROTEIN: ★★ FIBRE: ★★ CARBOHYDRATE: ★★★
VITAMINS: C, folic acid, E
MINERALS: K, Ca

Peach Ice

MAKES **8** 125 ml (4½ fl oz) Scoops

THIS goes well with the raspberry ice. It's not really worth making much less than this quantity, which is why each ice serves eight scoops. But it will keep in the freezer.

4 large ripe peaches	175 g (6 oz) half-fat crème fraîche or full-fat Greek yogurt
275 ml (½ pint) peach juice	
100 g (3½ oz) fruit sugar (fructose)	juice of ½ lemon

Peel, stone and chop the peaches and blend with the rest of the ingredients. Freeze as for Raspberry Ice.

NUTRITION

CALORIES PER PORTION (ONE 125 ML/4½ FL OZ SCOOP): 125
TOTAL FAT PER PORTION: 3.5 g
SATURATED FAT PER PORTION: 2.5 g

PROTEIN: ★ FIBRE: ★★ CARBOHYDRATE: ★★★
VITAMINS: C, beta-carotene, A
MINERALS: K

---

*B*raised Peaches with Strawberry Fool

SERVES 4

A NICE, easy dessert; the combination of peaches and creamy strawberry fool is quite divine.

4 ripe, but not overripe, peaches	125 g (4½ oz) strawberries
a little lemon juice	1 tablespoon fruit sugar (fructose)
100 ml (3½ fl oz) dessert wine	125 g (4½ oz) ricotta cheese

Preheat the oven to 180°C/350°F/Gas Mark 4. Halve the peaches and stone them, and brush the cut sides of the peaches with lemon juice. Place the peaches on a baking dish, cut-sides up, pour the wine over and cook in the oven for 15 minutes or until quite soft, but not mushy, when pierced with a skewer.

Meanwhile, reserve four of the strawberries and mash the rest with the sugar. Mix well with the ricotta. Serve the peaches very slightly warm, with any juices and with a spoonful of the strawberry fool in each cavity. Decorate each peach with a strawberry.

NOTES AND TIPS

✦ *You could use canned peaches in juice for this if you want to omit the braising stage. Just fill canned peach halves with the strawberry mixture. The calorie count will be 25 less per portion.*

NUTRITION

CALORIES PER PORTION: 145   PROTEIN: ★ FIBRE: ★★ CARBOHYDRATE: ★★★
TOTAL FAT PER PORTION: 4.5 g   VITAMINS: C, beta-carotene
SATURATED FAT PER PORTION: 2.5 g   MINERALS: K

Easy Summer Puddings

SERVES 4

THIS is probably the healthiest pud around – and one of the most delightful. A traditional summer pudding made in a basin is easy enough, but this is much quicker.

225 g (8 oz) blackcurrants, stalks removed	2 tablespoons fruit sugar (fructose)
110 g (4 oz) redcurrants, stalks removed	6 slices of brown bread from a cut loaf, crusts removed
325 g (12 oz) raspberries	

Put the fruits in a saucepan with 100 ml (3½ fl oz) water. Heat to simmering point, and barely simmer for just a few minutes or until the blackcurrants are beginning to burst their skins and the juices are running very freely.

Stir in the fructose until dissolved. Check for sweetness; if the mixture is very tart, add a little more fructose, but don't make it too sweet and cloying.

Cut each slice of bread into six. Put three pieces in each of four wide-necked wine glasses or stemmed dessert dishes. Spoon over some fruit and juice, then repeat with another layer of bread and fruit, finishing with three pieces of bread each. Spoon over the remaining juice and leave for 1–2 hours so that the bread gets soaked with juice.

NOTES AND TIPS

✦ *Serve with some low-fat Greek yogurt spooned on the top of each pudding, adding an extra 15 calories and 1 g fat per tablespoon.*

NUTRITION

CALORIES PER PORTION: 190　　PROTEIN: ★★ FIBRE: ★★★ CARBOHYDRATE: ★★★
TOTAL FAT PER PORTION: 1.5 g　　VITAMINS: C, B$_3$, E, beta-carotene, folic acid
SATURATED FAT PER PORTION: trace　　MINERALS: K, Fe, Ca

Shades of Red Fruit Salad

SERVES 4

AFTER a filling main course a pretty fresh fruit salad is always welcome.

1 medium pink grapefruit	125 g (4½ oz) strawberries, hulled and sliced if large
1 blood orange	
1 red-skinned apple	1 tablespoon fruit sugar (fructose)
175 g (6 oz) watermelon	250 ml (9 fl oz) light apple and summer berry fruit juice, or 125 ml (4½ fl oz) apple juice diluted with 125 ml (4½ fl oz) water
50 g (2 oz) seedless red or black grapes	
100 g (3½ oz) raspberries	

Peel the grapefruit and orange with a sharp, serrated knife, removing all the pith, then cut into segments, removing as much membrane and pith as you can. Do this over a plate to catch all the juices. Arrange the segments in a glass serving bowl with any juice.

Core and slice the apple, leaving the skin on, and mix with the grapefruit and orange. Cube the watermelon, removing the seeds, and add to the bowl with the grapes, raspberries and strawberries, then sprinkle over the fructose. Finally, pour the fruit juice over and chill, tossing once or twice, very gently, to combine the flavours. Serve chilled.

NOTES AND TIPS

✦ *Serve with low-fat Greek yogurt, adding 15 calories and 1 g fat per tablespoon, or 8 per cent fat fromage frais, adding 17 calories and 1.2 g fat per tablespoon.*

NUTRITION

CALORIES PER PORTION: 95

TOTAL FAT PER PORTION: 0.25 g

SATURATED FAT PER PORTION: trace

PROTEIN: ★ FIBRE: ★★ CARBOHYDRATE: ★★★

VITAMINS: C, beta-carotene, folic acid, E

MINERALS: K

Pears Poached in Red Wine

SERVES 4

ANOTHER easy dessert that, nevertheless, is impressive enough to serve at a dinner party.

4 ripe but firm pears	4 cloves
½ bottle (375 ml/12 fl oz) red wine	40 g (1½ oz) fruit sugar (fructose)
2.5 cm (1 inch) cinnamon stick	

Peel the pears, halve and core them. Put the pear halves in a saucepan or flameproof casserole with the wine, spices and fructose, and spoon the wine over the pears. Add enough water just to cover the pears. Cover the pan and simmer for 30 minutes or until the pears are tender.

Remove the pears from the pan with a slotted spoon and keep warm. Boil the liquid until reduced and thick. Remove the cinnamon and cloves. Arrange the pears in individual serving bowls and spoon the sauce over. Serve barely warm.

NOTES AND TIPS

✦ *You can keep the pears whole if you like and stand them on their fat ends in a pan. You may need to use more wine and water, or baste from time to time so that the pears turn red.*

NUTRITION

CALORIES PER PORTION: 130

TOTAL FAT PER PORTION: trace

SATURATED FAT PER PORTION: trace

PROTEIN: ★ FIBRE: ★★ CARBOHYDRATE: ★★★

VITAMINS: beta-carotene, E

MINERALS: K

Saint Clement's Pancakes

SERVES 4

PEOPLE seem to think that pancakes are 'naughty', but they're not really, especially if made with wholemeal flour and skimmed milk. They're full of minerals and fibre, and contain very little fat. Here's a delightful way to enjoy them for under 200 calories a portion.

2 oranges	pinch of salt
juice of 1 lemon	1 size-3 egg
1 tablespoon fruit sugar (fructose)	250 ml (9 fl oz) skimmed milk
110 g (4 oz) wholemeal flour	2 teaspoons groundnut oil

Peel the oranges and cut into segments with a sharp knife, removing as much pith and membrane as you can. Do this over a lipped board or plate to catch all the juices. Put the orange segments, juices, lemon juice and fructose in a bowl, stir well and set aside.

Sift the flour and salt into a mixing bowl, then add the contents of the sieve to the bowl, too. Make a well in the centre of the flour, add the egg, and beat, gradually incorporating the flour and adding the milk until you have a mixture that looks like thin cream. If you can, let the mixture stand for 30 minutes.

When you are ready to make the pancakes, heat the orange mixture in the microwave (1 minute on high) or in a saucepan for a few minutes and keep warm. Heat an omelette pan (see note) or small non-stick frying pan, and brush the bottom with a little of the oil. When really hot, swirl about one eighth of the pancake mixture into the pan to coat the bottom evenly. Cook for 1–2 minutes, then lift an edge of the pancake with a spatula to see if the underneath is golden. When it is, turn or toss the pancake and cook the other side for 1 minute. Remove to a warm plate and continue cooking the pancakes until you have cooked all eight.

You can either serve each person after two pancakes are cooked, with a quarter of the orange mixture spooned over, or you can pile the pancakes up as you make them, with greaseproof paper between each one, and keep them warm in the oven until you have cooked them all.

NOTES AND TIPS

✦ *It's best to keep a pan especially for cooking omelettes and pancakes. This should be no more than 18 cm (7 inches) in diameter, heavy-based and never washed, only wiped out with kitchen paper to retain a perfect non-stick surface which needs minimal fat.*

✦ *Pancakes should never be 'fried'; you only need a minute amount of oil to coat the pan, and the hotter the pan gets and the more pancakes you've cooked, the easier it will be to turn them out perfectly every time.*

NUTRITION

CALORIES PER PORTION: 190	PROTEIN: ★★★ FIBRE: ★★★ CARBOHYDRATE: ★★★
TOTAL FAT PER PORTION: 5 g	VITAMINS: B group, E, A, D, C
SATURATED FAT PER PORTION: 1 g	MINERALS: K, Mg, Fe, Zn, Ca

Brown Bread Ice Cream with Apricot Sauce

SERVES 4

HERE'S a quick way to turn plain vanilla ice cream into an interesting dessert. The crunchy pieces of bread and the tasty sauce make it a dessert enjoyed by young and old alike.

3 slices of slightly stale wholemeal bread, crusts removed
25 g (1 oz) caster sugar
500 ml (18 fl oz) low-calorie soft-scoop vanilla ice cream (e.g. Weight Watchers Real Dairy Ice Cream)
220 g (7½ oz) can apricots in juice

Preheat the oven to 180°C/350°F/Gas Mark 4.

Tear the bread into small pieces about 3–5 mm (⅛–¼ inch) square. Heat 3 tablespoons water in a saucepan, and add the sugar. Stir until the sugar has dissolved, then boil for a couple of minutes to reduce slightly. Add the bread to the pan, quickly stirring it round so that it is all coated with the syrup. Spread the pieces of bread out as well as you can on a baking sheet (they will be quite soggy but you need to spread them out as much as you can), and bake in the oven for 15 minutes or until the bread is golden and crisp. (Look at it every couple of minutes after the first 10 minutes because once it starts to colour it will soon char.) Leave on the baking sheet to cool.

Take the ice cream out of the freezer and soften it slightly. (A microwave on low will do this in 1 minute; otherwise you will have to leave it at room temperature for 20 minutes or so.)

Stir the bread into the ice cream, mixing well, then return the ice cream to the freezer to firm up a little again. Meanwhile, make the apricot sauce by simply whizzing the apricots with their juice in a blender for 20–30 seconds. Serve the ice cream with the sauce poured over.

NOTES AND TIPS

✦ *You can use fresh apricots, simmered in a little water, for the sauce, if you prefer, which will add more fibre to the dish.*

NUTRITION

CALORIES PER PORTION: 175	PROTEIN: ★ FIBRE: ★★ CARBOHYDRATE: ★★★
TOTAL FAT PER PORTION: 4 g	VITAMINS: B₃, beta-carotene
SATURATED FAT PER PORTION: 2 g	MINERALS: Ca, Fe, K

INDEX